A Little Bit
of
Pleasure

ME Sims

Want to know more? Visit www.ALittleBitOfPleasure.com

ISBN-13: 978-0996823005

Contents

My Disclaimer to the Reader

There is a sisterhood of women. However, we don't avail ourselves of the resources we possess. There is help out there for us. We can give each other courage, stability and, most of all, an understanding that goes beyond anything you can buy.

I'm just a regular woman, with the same experiences and anxieties as you. I believe women have been given bad information or no information about their bodies and sex. Our education stems from our mothers, the clergy, and so-called medical professionals. It's full of a hodgepodge of outdated statistics and theories.

In real life no one is addressing the issue of our bodies and our sex lives, unless it's about a man and his need to get a hard on! There is plenty of information on that topic.

The main question you're going to ask regarding this book is "Who the heck is ME Sims?" And "Why should I listen to what she has to say?" Well, I'm not a doctor or a sex therapist, but I do have these people at my fingertips. In fact, they have helped me write this book, Dr. Jerry and Dr. Richard.

Ladies from all over the United States have come to me through email, phone calls, retreats, seminars, and other women saying, "Call ME."

They have shared their frustrations, sorrows and successes with me, but the number one question I get is about SEX. The message

I want to share is: Sex can be fun. However, some of us have to learn how to make it delightful.

So let's get down to getting "A Little Bit of Pleasure" out of our lives.

—ME

Dedication

To all the women who asked questions and had the courage to change their lives.

The stories in this book are true; the names have been changed to protect the horny!

Chapter 1: Introduction

This book is for those of you who are over 40 and feel your sex life is over. Ladies, we still have half of our lives ahead of us. Instead of packing it in, let's be willing to reach out and fight for it. Your sex life is not extinguished, it's just hidden under a dump truck of bad experiences, personal issues, and a lack of knowledge about our bodies and how they work.

Because I am a woman, I have been told how to feel, what to feel, and how I feel for years. No matter what I thought, on almost any subject, I was told that I was wrong. I want other women who read this book to know they are not alone.

This book is centered on our sex lives. It's okay to be disappointed, frustrated, scared, fearful, shy, and totally confused about how you feel regarding sex. In the years of my research, I have read a lot of books on how women should feel about sex. Ninety percent of these books are written by men. I started my journey in my own sex education when I was about 40 years of age. I'm still learning.

This book is very personal and intimate. I will be sharing my sexual experience, my strength, and my hope with women who do not have the knowledge to guide them on how to have a happy sex life, especially if you're over 40. Well, here it goes!

❦

I think everybody has a desire for sex. Some people have very strong sex drives while others have a much lower level. On a scale of 1 to 10, I'm probably about a 15. I know people with desires higher than mine and people who are lower than that. I think that's all normal.

I was raised to think sex was sinful. The only reason to have sex was to procreate. When I was eight years old, my mother caught me masturbating in the bathtub. She told me that I was bad and I would be going to hell, which meant I would be a "crispy critter," but I didn't stop touching myself. Why? Because it felt too good! By the time I was an adult around age 20, I had figured it out. Why would I do anything different? I was going to hell anyway. That started my vicious cycle of shame, guilt, self-hate, and feelings of betrayal towards my body.

I didn't know what to do with myself because, at an early age, I had this feeling, this desire for something between my legs. I didn't know what it was, I didn't have any idea at all, but it was strong and I knew it was wrong.

I started my period when I was nine years old. My body started reacting to things a whole lot differently than the other girls I knew. I shared what happened to me with my best friend, Mary Jane. She told her mother and suddenly I was a "bad influence" and we couldn't play together anymore. I was treated like I had a disease; again I was bad.

The funny thing here, and it's truly funny, is that when I started my period my mom and dad were all excited because I was now a woman. That's what they told me. By the fourth grade I was in a 34B bra. My teacher called my parents and said that I needed a bra because my breasts jiggled and it was distracting. The teacher was a male. I wonder who really had the problem.

In sixth grade I was in parochial school and the nuns made fun of me because my breasts didn't fit right in the uniform. The uniform was a blue material with a "bib" which was designed for flat-chested girls. My breasts hung out the sides. That produced more shame and guilt because I was so different. As I got older, my body changed radically and I gained a lot of weight, almost 100 pounds.

I always wanted a huge family. That's all that I ever wanted in life—to be a mom, wife, and eventually a grandma. Those weren't the cards I was dealt. There is not one of us who has not had their share of heartbreak, disappointment, and sadness. I am now in my late 60s and I've had several completely different careers. Today, my life is amazing. I am extremely happy. Please let me know if yours turned out like you planned, or something worse or way better. My contact information is at the end of this book.

ᕙᕗ

All of my children were born early. My daughter was born eight months into my pregnancy;

my first son at seven months. With my third child, I was not aware I was pregnant until I was six months along. One of the reasons was because I was so overweight.

During the pregnancy I had gangrene of the intestines. My son was born during the seventh month of my pregnancy, but only lived for two and a half hours. He didn't survive due to the gangrene. It was recommended by my doctors that I should not have any more children.

What could I do? My religion said it was my job to have babies. I couldn't use protection because my religion said it was wrong. Therefore, I couldn't have sex. My husband did not believe in this; no one had the right to tell him how and when to have sex. So I got pregnant again only seven months after losing our son. This child was also born seven months into the pregnancy and almost died. A very loving and kind priest came to me and said, "You can NOT have any more children." Here's another strange fact: since this priest said that I couldn't have any more children, it was OKAY, because we know all priests are gods (aren't they?) and messengers on earth, right? Well, that took care of that! I could never have any more children. You would think my burden of guilt and shame was lifted. But it wasn't.

Let me tell you, I was plagued with such guilt and shame. I felt I was no longer of any value because I could not produce children. On the other hand, I wanted to do a happy dance and was filled with delight because now I could have sex and I didn't have to worry about getting pregnant. It was a double-edged sword that kept stabbing me over and over again. I felt so incredibly bad because I only had three living children.

My sister, in contrast, had a ton of kids. I felt so inferior and worthless every time I was around her. No wonder I weighed over 220 pounds at the age of 28, and I'm short to boot. (At that time, I looked like a pumpkin, the only thing missing was I wasn't orange). Soon after that, I joined a weight-reducing program, which enabled me to lose the weight and deal with what I was eating over.

I believe guilt is a useless emotion, unless we use it to change ourselves to become better people: The person I wanted to be, not what they said I had to be. There is a saying, "When all else fails, use guilt!" Guilt and shame are emotions, which enable other people to control us. John Bradshaw is a great author on this subject, "Healing the shame that binds you." I recommend his books. Check out my recommended reading guide at the end of this book.

Remember, I am not a doctor. I don't profess to know all the ins and outs of the human mind, but I do know the human soul. Mine was incomplete and in total torment. I could tell you all of my deep, dark secrets. I can tell you all kinds of things about my family. I could argue politics and religion. But I couldn't talk about sex to anyone. During the sexual revolution, the flower children, Woodstock, and sex-drugs-and-rock-n-roll, I secretly wanted to be a part of that life, wild and free, all the while I condemned anyone who followed it. Today there is no condemnation in me anymore for anything or anyone or any way you want to live.

Please join me on this exciting adventure.

Chapter 2:
Initiation into The Man's World

Once upon a time long long ago in the land of milk and honey and sweetness and light, I was a preschool teacher. I dealt with cute little kids and their doting parents. Then one day my life changed and I had to get a different job... in a completely different universe.

In 1989, I was 42 years old, single, and I was starting work at one of the largest dealerships in the United States, as a car salesman!

In those days were weren't salespeople. They called us salesmen. That's the way it was. I had no experience whatsoever. I had $6.00 to my name after I had scraped together my nickels to buy a dress for the interview.

I was the new girl on the block, in fact the entire block. When I started, we had 75 salesmen and 2 women. However, the other lady was in the commercial accounts department. We could not wear pants, because we were ladies. I walked the lot in heels and a dress. Hey ladies, how about a high five for courage and determination!

It was really a different world in a lot of ways. It was all about men. I was older than my bosses and 20 years older than most of the men who were on my sales team. It was quite a culture shock for me. I think for them too.

The way they talked, the way they walked, what they talked about, their body language was all foreign to me. They would scratch anywhere at any time without giving any care to who was around to watch. So many times I thought they were just tall four year olds because if they were waiting for the next person to come in to buy a car and they had to go to the bathroom they would shift back and forth just like a four year old who didn't want to stop playing to go pee.

I had been there only maybe three months and I was doing quite well considering I knew nothing about selling cars. The people liked me and people do business with people they like so I won a big dealership contest. I was able to go on a winter retreat with the guys. There were probably about 30 of us and they brought their wives and their girlfriends. It was really a great, fun time. However...

My team and I were on snowmobiles having a wonderful time. On our way back to the lodge, just before getting off the snowmobile, one of the young men grabbed me off the snowmobile, threw me to the ground, and straddled me. The men who were watching, all five of them, all under the age of 25, were laughing their heads off! The young man got off me, turned around, and walked towards his friends. The guys were still laughing and high fiving each other. I was pissed but I didn't know what the hell to do. I walked up, grabbed the man by the back of his coat collar, and pulled him backwards to the ground. (I outweighed him by 30 pounds.) I straddled him, grabbed him by the front of his coat, and said, "Don't you ever pick on a grandma again!" with a smile. With that, I got off him. He put his arm around me and said, "You're all right, Sims." From that moment on I was one of the boys. I had passed the test.

❧

New salesmen were called "Green Ps" when they were fresh on the floor. I'm a pretty good sport and I don't have thin skin but I know what's right and I know what's wrong, and one particular day I was standing at the counter when one of the boys came up from behind and put his arm around my body, covering my chest with his forearm. He squeezed me really tightly and it hurt my breasts. I pushed him away and called him an asshole. He laughed as the other boys watched. (I thought I had already passed my initiation.) I pushed him away and turned around and left the scene. I walked into the boss's office and said, "If that son of a bitch ever touches me again, I'm going to own your ass and his too! Do I make myself clear?" Our boss just looked at me and I walked out of his office. I had already proven myself on the skiing trip, and this was going a little too far. I didn't know if he got my message. My boss was only 30, maybe 35, but that would be pushing it.

The following day I walked into my boss's office to discuss a car deal I was working on. I was sitting in front of him in a skirt with my legs crossed. One of the other guys on my team walked in. As he crossed in front of me to get to the other chair to my left, he grabbed my ankle. My boss saw this and jumped up out of his chair and yelled, "Don't touch her body!!!!" That poor salesman didn't know what had happened, but I guess my boss had gotten my message. That same salesman and I continued for many years to joke about the very incident because he didn't know why the boss was so upset. But I did, and that is all that mattered. The word got around that I did pass the test, and the word was I could take care of business.

Moving forward, it's now 1995 or 1996. I've been at the dealership for many years and am now part of management. I was part of the training team that educated the Green Ps on the care and feeding of upset customers, which was my specialty. I had a fancy title, I had a fancy staff, and I had a lot of people working under me.

But on this fine lovely day there was a salesman whom I call "Jack." He was black, 6 foot 6 inches, and 350 pounds. He could've stopped a Mack truck. He was leaning up against one of the vehicles on the showroom floor and he had a couple of the boys standing around him. As

I was walking by, I said, "Hey, Jack." He took a swing and slapped me on my ass. I turned around so fast. I looked at him in the eye and said, "If you ever put your black hand on my ass again without my permission I will own your fucking soul," and walked away. There was never a problem again. I know he was embarrassed, but I did not humiliate him, and I think there is a difference! Even in school, the boys pulled our ponytails. Don't ask me why it's the way it is. But it always comes down to how I react to any given situation. And I have learned to check my motives, check the reason why and, most importantly, I choose my battles. Remember that was 1996. Some things have changed, God I hope so!

∽

In my opinion, little boys grow up to be bigger little boys. I just love the little curl in the middle of their foreheads. When they're bad, they are so so bad, but when they're good, "mmmmm" they're so good.

But they are not going to push me around, and that still stands today.

Chapter 3:
God, Sex, & the Myths

Before you read this chapter, I suggest that you sit down with a glass of wine. I needed a glass to write it! I will be talking about a subject you probably don't want to hear or talk about.

Hopefully it will give you pause to think about some of the things we believe to be true and cut in stone; however, those thoughts, myths, and rules stop us from having *A Little Bit of Pleasure* in our lives.

ॐ

Myths we are taught about sex
I was in the bookstore today. I picked up a couple of books on exotic reading for a client of mine, and wedged between these books was a pamphlet on how Jesus saves sinners. Someone had to have placed that pamphlet between the books I was selecting, just to let anyone who picked up the book know that we were wrong, in their opinion.

My initial thought was, no wonder we are all screwed up about sex! My next thought was, "I'm wrong for looking at this." That thought didn't last long. Old thinking, pashaw!

ॐ

We have people, primarily men-run churches, telling us women what we can do, what we can't do, how we can do it, when we can do it, who we can do it with, how we better do it this way, and we better listen to this person. And if we don't or if we think those thoughts, we are bad. We're sinners and we're going to go to hell. Or take the government, mostly run by men, deciding on women's health issues. In some of the Southern states, it is still illegal to purchase a vibrator. In 2015? Really?

As young children, we never get to choose what to believe, but we believed to be true all the information which was passed down to us from our family and school and church and friends. We have trust in our parents and our teachers and our ministers because in our eyes as children they are gods and they can't do anything wrong. We accept their decisions for us because we know they wouldn't hurt us. We didn't get to choose anything, but we took their belief system and made it our own. Trying to leave that way of thinking is so difficult. You are considered an outcast by many.

Some of us kept our belief structures. In my years with working with women, the number one belief system that they have to overcome is about SEX. And SEX is tangled up with GOD. It's a hard chain to break.

Anne Lindburgh said, "Doubts and fears are the bars on my windows." It's been quite an experience looking at my own belief system and coming to grips with what wasn't true for me. That it doesn't mean that it's not true for somebody else. But I had to look at what was really true in me, and that was not easy. It has been a very interesting journey, but because I did put my beliefs under a microscope and I did search out different answers, I'm pretty healthy today in my convictions, whether they be about God, sex, religion, or politics. I've learned to form my own opinions and, yes, it was not what everybody else believed.

&

The United States of America has the most suppressed sexual history in the world. Just look around and compare us to other countries in the world. Where they have freedoms, they have freedom in sex. Sex is not a sin. (Forget the Middle East. That's a whole other story.) These beliefs really do shape our sexual habits.

There are so many religions in the United States of America and throughout the world. Let's talk about some of the major ones that primarily dole out guilt and shame: Catholic, Protestant, Muslim, Baptist, Mormon, Jehovah's Witness, and "Holy Rollers." Their view on sex is plain. You're not allowed to do it unless you're married, and you can't touch yourself (period). Here's an example of one Baptist woman's experience.

She wanted her Baptist friend to know that the use of a vibrator and other sex toys was allowable under their religion. The Baptist friend replied, "Only if it's used by your husband; you cannot use it by yourself. The husband is to be the source of all sexual pleasure."

If that were true in my case, I never would have had a decent sexual experience. I can't blame my three husbands because they didn't know how to provide such experiences. What I find fault with to this day is that some men are unwilling to learn or try something new or to have fun. I had a man tell me that he was enough for his wife. She didn't need anything else!

&

Back to the original subject. I do sometimes prattle on, so please forgive me.

In some sects of Mormonism their undergarments are blessed in the temple. They are worn under their clothes to keep the outside world from defiling their holy temple, their bodies.

Judaism teaches that a man and woman should please each other. That's the belief of most reform Jews; however, not of the orthodox Jew. In her book, *Unorthodox,* Deborah Feldman tells her own personal story as she lived it. In one part in the book, she explains that a father killed his six-year-old son because he caught him masturbating. Also she writes, after a woman is married she is to shave her head and wear a wig. The reason this is done is because the woman's real hair, cascading down from her head, might tempt another man to want her, causing him to sin. I think I got whiplash reading this because I kept shaking my head in disbelief. It's a look into another world right here today. Anyway, it's a great read.

There is a theme throughout the history of womanhood. We tempt them; it's always our fault. In the beginning, Adam got himself in a jam and blamed it on Eve. Well, I'm not buying it anymore.

Perhaps you've heard of the female mutilation of women's genitals in Africa. The vagina is sewn closed until the wedding ceremony. In some places, starting as an infant, the clitoris is mutilated or removed altogether. This is so they are not tempted to enjoy or have sex. Enjoyment is for their husbands.

I'm not bashing religion. In fact, I believe what George Carlin said, "Religion is like a pair of shoes... Find one that fits you, but don't make me wear your shoes."[1]

> ∾

QUESTION: Why is the world of men so afraid of women having good enjoyable sex? I ask you, why do you think that is?

These following statements are all true. The names have been changed to protect those women who dared to share them. After all, this book was written to protect the brave and the horny.

> ∾

♥ Barbara was sitting in a chair waiting for her friend to get ready to go play. She had her hands between her legs because she was cold. Sarah's mother came into the room and yelled, "Barbara, get your hands out from down there." Barbara didn't know what she had done wrong, but she now knew that down there was bad.

♥ You cannot wear patent leather shoes. If you do, the boys will be able to see up your skirt and see your panties.

♥ When I started dating, my mother gave me this advice, "Don't give a man a stiff prick." I thought, what's a prick?

♥ You cannot get your hair wet and go outside. It will stop your period.

♥ After childbirth you cannot wash your hair for two months. It's bad for the baby's milk.

♥ If you are not a virgin when you get married, there will be a black mark on your wedding dress and everyone will know.

♥ Sex is all the male species wants. Don't do it.

♥ My daddy told me never to give a man "blue balls" (which means to be a tease and not give him sex).

♥ My mother told me, "Pick a room in the house and perfect it. Now, sweetie, mine is not the kitchen." (I think I would've liked that mom. Unfortunately, this young lady didn't know what mom was talking about until after she was married.)

♥ Women are far more willing to accept a lousy sex life because they don't know any better.

♥ On my wedding day, my mommy said, "Now honey, when it comes time to do IT, you're probably gonna have to help him put it in. After that, he'll know what to do."

♥ Mom gave me a book on sex. She told me to go into my room and read it by myself. That was my sex education. We never discussed it.

♥ In my household, we never talked about sex, politics, or religion. Those subjects were taboo.

♥ She was three months shy of 10 years old. On day, while sitting on the toilet, her little brother saw blood in her panties. He ran from the bathroom, yelling "Jane bleeding, Jane is bleeding, she bleeding." Her mother came in and went out yelling to her dad, "SHE'S A WOMAN." Then the talk came. Mother simply said, "Now you can have a baby, so stay away from boys." Talk over!

♥ She was 14 years old and still secretly sucked her thumb. Grandma came in and caught her. Grandma said, "Are you going to be sucking your thumb when your boyfriend is fucking you"?

♥ She was 13, getting ready for the beach, and she spotted blood. Her mother gave her a Kotex to put on. Her dad came in and said, "I hear you're a woman now." Nothing more was said and off to the beach they went.

♥ Sue started her period at 11. She was so ashamed that she hid it from her mother for months. Sue would steal pads from her mother. Her father never commented on her ever-changing body. She was flooded with guilt and shame. From the church and friends, all she was told was to be a good girl and do not get pregnant.

♥ She was 14 and wanted to know about tampons. A girlfriend gave her one and told her that she had 2 holes and it went in the first one. She could not find it so she gave up.

∽

When I was in my "why stage" and searching for answers (which was most of my life), I asked a Protestant minister, "If sex is not to be enjoyed by both parties, why did God make it so enjoyable?" You're going to love his answer, and I promise you it's the truth! He stood facing me, with his hands on my shoulders, looking into my eyes, all spiritual-like, and he said, "So, my dear, that we may be tempted and learn to struggle against the temptation. In so doing we show our devotion to God."

The point I'm trying to make is that all this information floats around and is taught in one form or another, or sometimes we just pick it up. Then it gets lodged in our brains and we adopt it and make it ours. It is hard to remove it, whether it is true or right for us or not. We let it shape our sex lives, and we pass it on. Changing these belief systems is hard. I think most of the stuff I was taught were lies. Surprise! What if we're all wrong?

I would love to hear your stories!

Chapter 4:
The Toolbox

This Toolbox was designed to give women power tools to help them figure out what's going on inside and outside of their bodies. Not many of us have the luxury of existing in the jet set world (which truly exists only in realms of book fantasies) where servants take care of our every whim. Most of us live in the real world with real jobs, real children, and real partners. The world of soccer, cooking, grocery shopping, dance, and I'll scrub the toilets on the weekend because I can't afford a house-keeper—or a therapist. Who is going to get it done? YOU!

And now someone wants sex. Put it on the list as something else you have to do. Some women will say okay. Others might think, "I'm too damn tired," and just lay there or fake it. Yep, we do fake it. While 75 percent of men reach orgasm during sex, only 29 percent of women report the same. In addition, most women are unable to climax through vaginal intercourse alone, needing clitoral stimulation instead.[2]

That's a bummer. Are you thinking, "When is it my turn?" It's now! You have to take control of your own sex life. Let's go back to the toolbox. Here are the tools you might want to grab as we head out on this adventure: An Open Mind, Pen and Paper, and a Willingness to try something new and different—and don't forget the wine. First, look at your belief system concerning sex. Write down the hurdles in your path that keep you from enjoying it. A big step for many women is ridding ourselves of shame and guilt. Another step is the willingness to share intimately. You also need an Open Mind. Yep, I already said that, but it might have closed shut again!

The Toolbox and exercises enclosed are designed specifically to get to the heart of the problem, if you want to call it that. Also, the other neat thing about this Toolbox is that it comes with your own personal therapist and solutions you can try at home. There is no time frame and no installation is required. You will be able to create a new you. That is, if you want it. (Take a moment to pause and think on that.) How is the glass of wine holding out?

∾

Keep in mind that you're not alone anymore. I was alone for a long time before I got any help or answers. The answers eventually came from me, deep down in my soul. It took some serious work. I had to be truthful with myself. But I really wanted a better sex life and an all-around better life. It took a while but I came to realize that no one else was going to give me what I needed besides me. It may take a little time for you also. You might be thinking, "Yeah, they all say that." But it is possible.

What do you really want? Keep that Open Mind! Be real. It's not easy being real, but being realistic is the first step. I said, "I WANT someone else to do the housework, cooking, etc." Once I figured out what I wanted, I was able to act on it. I started delegating. Didn't God give us children to do the dishes? And take out the trash? Well yes, God did. So I started there.

Here's my guilt voice. My mother said, "If you want something done, do it yourself." Well, that almost killed her, and guilt was going to kill me. (You will find Guilt Removal in the Toolbox.) Delegating chores was harder in the beginning, but it worked, bit by bit. I could not expect it to be done exactly like I would have done it, especially my husband's part. If they did it, I had to try to be happy that they had tried. It was a process, slow but steady.

If you do not have children, then delegate the chores for another night. Not everything has to be done at the same time. I had an invisible timekeeper inside my head: Things had to be done NOW and done in a certain way. No wonder I was too tired to have sex. We struggle with this, don't we, ladies?

Don't be a shape shifter. I had been conforming to fit the people (most of all men) in my life. This was not their fault. It was mine— mine and my insecurities. I felt so little about myself and didn't think I had any value. I used to wonder why I didn't have any talent or smarts. I just became the woman they wanted. Like me, love me, then I will be okay! I was too afraid to stand on my own. My belief system was broken. The same tapes played in my head over and over. This is why I called it the Shape Shifter. I became what they wanted because of my lack of confidence in my future. I was terrified that someone would be mad at me or yell or get angry with me. I performed certain sex acts because that's what they wanted, not because I wanted to.

At age 35 I started to stand up for myself. It was a hard process for me, but the more I tried to listen to what was important to me the better I got at it. This was my turning point: I had just had TMJ surgery on my jaw. I was instructed by the doctor not to overtax my jaw, to let it rest and heal. But my husband wanted a blowjob and wanted me to swallow. I hated doing that, always did. Not the blowjob, just the swallowing part. After four years of obeying at his insistence, I said NO. I didn't like it and hated the taste. (The taste depends on the food men eat—junk food certainly creates a lousy taste.) When I said NO, I closed my eyes and waited for the heavens to open up and all hell to break loose. But my husband was a bully in words only. Because I stood up and refused to swallow, we were able to make the blow job a part of OUR sex life, not just his sex life. Remember, baby steps. You can make a change. I promise.

Fear Remover is another tool in the box. "Fear is a thief that steals your day." Anonymous

I cannot count the women who have told me they would like to change their hair color or style, or something like that. But NO, they can't, because their husband, mother, or boyfriend wants it this way and they think, "If I change it they will get mad at me. It's just not worth the hassle." Have you said those words? Is there anything you might want to change? Well I had things I wanted to change. More than I can count.

One day I got fed up and wanted my hair different. My long, curly hair was too much work and too costly. I had it cut to shoulder length and I loved it. It felt great. My husband didn't like it at first, but after a week, to my surprise, he told me, "Hey, your hair looks nice that way." I almost fell over. This new tool of Taking Care of Me was wonderful. The big truth and little secret is that when I really mean no, or when I'm not going to put up with unacceptable behavior, the people know I mean it and they sense I'm speaking from a point of power. It was a wonderful discovery. I didn't tell anybody that the jig was up; I just figured it out.

Yes, I was scared to try it again, but each time I got better at expressing myself. Going to the movies by myself to see a chick flick, or even having lunch with a girlfriend, made me feel like I was sinning. As a child and young adult I never saw my mother going out with a girlfriend. She really did not have girlfriends. How sad for her.

Using the tools (even the battery operated ones) in the Toolbox helped me change my life.

I'm just like all of you, my sisters. We just don't look alike. Remember the sisterhood!

By the way, there is an organization called Chemo Chicks.[3] They are a great example of the sisterhood of women. My motto now is, Anything is Possible, "the impossible takes a little longer."[4]

Chapter 5:
Weight & Sex

Okay, I know you're saying to yourself, "Where in the hell is she going to go with this weight crap?" In my old overeating life I had sex so you would like me and love me and care for me. When I was fat, if anyone gave me any attention, which was not often, I figured I had to love them because they actually wanted to go to bed with fat ol' me. My weight never stopped me from having sex and I was never told by a man, "Hey, you're too fat to have sex with," but it made a difference inside me. It didn't affect my capabilities in having sex, but instead it affected my ability to have pure un-restricted fun and joy. What was missing was freedom, freedom from guilt and shame. I had pure hatred for my own body, which didn't measure up in my mind. I always compared myself to impossibly beautiful women on tele-vision or in the movies. Most of all, I lacked respect for myself. I was ashamed of how my body looked naked. I knew that if any man looked at me, he would be repulsed by my body.

After I lost weight and went from a size 22 to a size 10-12, for the first time in my life I felt pretty, attractive, and desirable. Especially that last word: DESIRABLE. It almost put me over the edge. I wanted to run to the nearest all-you-can-eat smorgasbord and put all my weight back on! The reason was a little convo-luted, but this is how I really felt. Even though I looked different on the outside, I still had the same old fat thinking going on inside. I still thought that if I got attention from a man, I must act on it. And because I wanted to act on it, I was filled with guilt because that would make me a whore.

I had never in my life felt attractive. My mother had told me, "You have such a pretty face, BUT… " Yes, that big "but." I just knew that I was fat and stupid and the only thing I was good for was to make babies. Once I reached the point where I couldn't have any more babies, I really struggled with my self-worth. I never imagined being put in this dilemma of becoming a sexy woman and all that comes with that blessing/curse.

One day around this particular time in my life, a man I knew picked me up, swirled me around with my feet off the ground, and exclaimed, "You are beautiful!" I was so scared I pushed him away from me awkwardly. I said to him in a loud voice, "My husband is perfect!" He looked at me with a big smile on his face and laughed. He got it. He knew I was scared to death. He didn't do it to make me scared. He did it because he was being sincere. He thought I was beautiful and wanted me to know it. I could not handle that!

I told a friend how I was feeling and how scared I was. I asked her, "What does that mean? What do I do?" And all the gibberish that was running through my head like a train. She stated gently, "ME you do not have to act on those, they are just feelings. Feelings aren't right or wrong or good or bad… they just… are." That is the sisterhood of us women at work.

And that day I got a full understanding of the recovery process and living healthy. I could make a grown-up decision based on what was best for me, not letting a feeling make it for me. Whether it was food or sex, I had choices now, not compulsions. There was such freedom in acknowledging the feelings I was experiencing but not letting them determine the course of my life.

There really is a secret hell that women like me, who lose a lot of weight and become attractive, go through. We don't know how to deal with sexual feelings—from others or from ourselves. It frightens us. Toss in a disgruntled husband or a parent who says "You don't look so good anymore, you're too skinny." Or your girlfriends who are jealous because you've lost weight and they haven't. That's when the "friendly fire" comes from people close to you trying to bombard and sabotage you.

For some of us, it's just easier to go back to the old life of eating and being fat, where everyone we trusted seemed to like us more. The saboteurs come out when we start to lose weight. Living healthy can open a Pandora's Box of new issues to deal with, especially if your husband is insecure about himself, because… You're not going to like what I'm going to say. Maybe you'd better get a glass of wine and sit down.

Are you comfy?

Here's the unvarnished truth from someone who has lived it herself: Some men marry fat women because they think nobody else wants them. These men think they don't have to work at keeping their wife happy because some of us will put up with anything rather than be alone. And best of all for these men, their wife's fat is a great barrier. It keeps people from getting close to them, especially men on the prowl. This is true for a lot of women who have been sexually molested or abused by a man and are keeping men away by using fat as a shield. This has been my experience. Other women put up with this kind of behavior because it's easier to let someone else take care of them. I did that myself as well. Okay, drink up, because more is coming.

∾

A huge yardstick for growth with a big mirror looking back at me was on my 43rd birthday, when I was still working at the dealership. I had worked bell to bell which means open to close, I was tired, it was late, and I didn't have time to eat my dinner. And I felt I was going nowhere. At 43, nothing in my life had worked out how I wanted it to. My plans were for the white picket fence, the apron, and a house full of kids. Now I was old enough to be a grandma and that wasn't happening. My kids were not perfect and I was on my second divorce. I felt like I was a huge failure as a wife and mother, and with all this, the whole day of my 43rd birthday sucked.

I ended up at a Denny's diner to get my free birthday dinner and it didn't even taste good. I came home and called the only friend I thought I had. As I talked, she listened. Then she reminded me all that had taken place in exactly one year. I had moved and then found out my husband was stealing and cheating on me. I quit my day job and went to work for a big car dealership. Then I turned 43. She said to me very gently, "You know, ME, you might be grieving for the life you thought you were going to have."

With that statement the floodgates opened. I slid down the wall (which had been holding me up), and sat on the floor and cried my eyes out. With clarity of mind I came to realize this was the truth, the unadulterated truth. No touch-up paint, no makeover; not a pretty picture. I was grieving, grieving for the life I thought I was supposed to have.

∾

Please don't feel sorry for me. Besides, I don't want you crying in your glass of wine. I hate watered down wine! This was just a real consciousness I was not aware of until it hit. Then I was able to look squarely in the eye of reality and say, "Okay, let's start on a new adventure!"

Today I can look back on that 43rd birthday and joke about it. I like to say that, with my first husband I got my bachelor's degree, with my second husband I got my master's degree, but with my third husband, I got my doctorate in Life Studies. Through it all I ended up liking myself, respecting myself, and enjoying my own company. And today I can share this with you, the one with the aching heart. I want you to know you're not alone. There's somebody here for you who will listen and help the best way that they possibly can. Please don't give up on you. I won't. I'm your cheerleader.

Chapter 6:
Sexual Headache

What in the world is a sexual headache? There is something like that and it's real. The clinical name is coital headache or coital cephalagia.

Coital cephalalgia is a headache condition that occurs during sexual intercourse. It is caused by an adrenaline rush to the brain. Sex headaches are brought on by sexual activity, especially an orgasm. You may notice a dull ache in your head and neck that builds up as sexual excitement increases. Or more commonly, you may experience a sudden, severe headache just before or during orgasm.

Most sex headaches are nothing to worry about, but some can be a sign of something serious, such as problems with the blood vessels that feed your brain. Sex headaches aren't usually a cause for concern. However, you should consult your doctor right away if you experience a headache during sexual activity—especially if it begins abruptly or it's your first headache of this type.

There are two types of sexual headaches.

The most common variety:
Gives no warning and occurs within a few seconds of an orgasm
Is often described as throbbing or stabbing
Can happen to men and women

The other variety of sexual headache:
Often begins as a dull ache on both sides of the head

May cause tightening of the neck and jaw muscles

Builds gradually over a matter of minutes before an orgasm

Intensifies as sexual excitement increases

Can happen to men and women

In my case, it started with an incredible SHARP pain which shot to the top of my head. It began at the onset of a climax (which could prevent you from continuing to climax or having one). I believe mine was caused by the increased adrenaline rush and extreme intense excitement. I only had it one time and it lasted over 45 minutes. The pain slowly subsided but left me exhausted. It scared both my partner and me.

What we did was I lay still and he put cold towels on my head. Later that day I did call the doctor. My head hurt, but it hurt like a sore muscle. He told me to go to the hospital right away. They did a spinal tap. They feared I had an aneurysm. But I just had a sexual headache. I had never heard of this and with all the people I have spoken to and all the books I have read, I found nothing, so I put it to the Internet and found all I could and more. I still have great sex but have not had a headache since.

A year later I received a call from a man in his 40s. He had a sexual headache. I explained all of the above to him. He went to the doctor and they found nothing. However, they suggested he go on beta-blockers. He didn't like the feeling of the drug because it dulled his senses, but as of this writing he has not had another headache since.

Here is some information for your Tool Box. Dr. David and Dr. Dee from Med Help International stated, "The first, and most common [type of sexual headache], is the benign coital headache," which tends to occur on a regular basis during or after sex, and is relatively harmless. This headache tends "to occur before or during an orgasm, and may persist for a period of minutes, or hang on for hours after sex. It can occur in both men and women. Although benign coital or orgasmic headaches are very painful, and obviously limit sexual enjoyment, they present no other acute threat. They are thought to result from muscle contraction, and/or blood vessel dilation, in the head and neck during sex."[5]

The second type is the "new onset severe headache during sex." This is a first time headache, which is generally characterized as the worst headache ever. This type of sex headache is a serious emergency until proven otherwise. This could be caused by a brain hemorrhage or other similar condition.

Fortunately, this type of first onset headache is fairly unusual, but when it does occur it can represent a life-threatening emergency that requires emergency evaluation and treatment. A brain hemorrhage may occur during sex when an abnormal blood vessel *bursts*, causing an acute hemorrhage over the surface of the brain, or within the brain. Brain bleed comprises only a tiny percentage of all headaches, but if not diagnosed and treated immediately the result can be catastrophic.

That's why doctors maintain a high index of suspicion about an explosive onset severe headache and why anyone with such a headache needs an emergency evaluation by a physician.

Chapter 7:
Menopause & Me

Menopause does not have to bring your life to a screeching halt, nor is your life extinguished. All of us women over the age of 40 eventually deal with the reality of menopause. Some experience it sooner than others, but it is as certain as taxes. Whether you are there now or not, I want to let you know what's coming and what is out there to help you be your own advocate. This way you can make your own decisions and overcome bad advice from well-meaning so-called experts like mom, myths, wives tales... and we can add to that list all day long. My wish for you is sexual health for your mind and body. And a whole lot of pleasure!

For many women menopause is synonymous with misery, but I do have good news: It doesn't have to be that way. Life can begin after menopause.

I started menopause at around 50-ish, and everything was so-so for a long while. Then things really started to change. I suffered from the following symptoms:

1. Moodiness
2. Sleeplessness (don't they use sleep deprivation as torture in other countries?)
3. Bitchiness
4. Extra belly fat
5. Emotional outbursts
6. Crying (too often over silly things)
7. Lack of sexual desire (don't touch me)

8. Vaginal dryness
9. Painful intercourse (my skin was so thin it look like it was burned around the outside and inside of the lips)
10. Thinning skin all over
11. Road rage (Men do not know what real road rage is. Try it on menopause!)

Like many other women, as I experienced this change of life I was flying blind about what was happening. Finally I got fed up and decided to find out what was going on and if I was the only one experiencing such severe symptoms.

I belong to a women's book club. I decided to take an informal poll, asking if my friends if they were going through the same thing. We were all over 45. Out of ten women, eight of us were in the same boat. Two of the ladies were on Bio-Identical Hormone Replacement Therapy, but I discounted this idea because it sounded like a lot of money, which I didn't have. Instead, I sought out regular medical relief for my various maladies.

My first experience talking about my symptoms was at age 55 with my male general practice physician. He told me it was normal and there was nothing he could do for me. He said menopause would last about 15 years and "it is not that bad, it is just nature taking its course. Just accept it." He told me to exercise and drink plenty of water. (Today, I would not let anyone talk to me that way.)

Unsatisfied with my GP, I next sought out advice from my female gynecologist. I assumed she knew and would understand about menopause. I told her I was bitchy and crying at the drop of a hat. I explained I was waking up at 2:30AM, my mind racing with all sorts of ideas and projects such as wanting to paint the house (inside and out), rearrange the furniture, or wanting to bake a batch of cookies for the kids (even though the kids were all grown up and lived in other states). At 2:30AM all those ideas seemed perfectly reasonable.

I begged her to give me something to help me sleep before I killed someone. I was so tired. She laughed at me and said, "Welcome to menopause. It is part of being a woman. And no, I won't give you sleeping pills." But she did tell me to take two Benzedrine at night to combat the sleeplessness symptoms. They did work, but the rest of my life continued with persistent misery. Now I really felt let down and depressed. Not even my female gynecologist could deliver me from my menopause mania. Once again I was told it was no big deal.

Because of other female problems, I was referred to Dr. G, a wonderful male gynecologist. He told me the American Medical Association and the big pharmaceutical companies have spent billions of dollars on research and development for getting a man's penis hard and very little money on women's health issues. I'm talking bazillions of dollars. I told him about my issues and that I wanted to try Bio-Identical Hormone Replacement Therapy.

He agreed but said all he could give me was the standard pills, kind of a generic one size fits all. Dr. G stated, "Most insurance companies will not pay for hormone therapy for women." We talked for 45 minutes; the nurse had to knock on the door and remind him he had other patients that were waiting. I tried the over the counter menopause stuff. All it did for me was lighten my pocketbook.

When sharing my story with the Book Club ladies, one recommend former "Three's Company" star Suzanne Somers' book, "The Sexy Years." I read it. Everything sounded great, but I did not have the same income as Susan and her doctor was in Beverly Hills. So I gave up. I didn't really want to suffer anymore, but no money, no way. I think that's the way it is for a lot of us. No extra money so there isn't a way.

As I was skipping down the road of menopause, my symptoms worsened. The one I hated the most was the dryness and the do-not-touch-me attitude. In fact, sex not only hurt but semen burned the walls of my vagina. I'm thinking, "What the hell? What in the world is wrong with me?" I'm too young to pack it up and stop feeling good and enjoying sex. I got this bright idea to ask my local health food vitamin store. I asked them if they knew someone who could help who might be local. They did and I made the call to the doctor. At this point I didn't care that I had to pay out of pocket. I think when you hit a bottom you'll do whatever you need to do. That's what happened to me and that's how I found Dr. Edward S. Hanzelik, MD in Westlake, CA.

Dr. Hanzelik ran a blood test and found I was depleted of hormones. A week later I started on the hormones made just for me. Dr. Hanzelik stated it would take about six weeks to see a difference. For me, it was three weeks. The first thing I noticed was I was horny. Yeah! I was having that lovin' feeling. Holy Moly! I had not felt this way for a year. And having sex did not hurt! Then I noticed my nails looked better. My skin and hair thinness and the night sweats were almost gone. The house still needed painting, but I no longer had obsessive thoughts about painting it at 2:30AM. Sometimes I still wake up early, but it might be two times a month, not every night. My peace of mind has returned. I don't feel like a loose squirrel in a cage. I feel 20 years younger. My mood has been lifted. What a wonderful feeling.

This is the timeline of my search for pain-less sex:

1. Regular GP when I was 50ish 2000-2003
2. Again the GP years later, same doctor, 2006-2007
3. Female gynecologist 2009
4. Dr. G, gynecologist, 2010
5. Dr. Hanzelik, the Bio-Identical Hormone Specialist, 2011

I continue to see my Dr. Hanzelik once a year for a blood test and general checkup. I still have to contend with being older but I sure don't feel it or act like it. I feel great. Life is good.

For Your Information:

Replens, an estrogen free vaginal moisturizer
www.replens.com

Replens Long-Lasting Vaginal Moisturizer provides immediate alleviation of dryness symptoms[6] and helps replenish vaginal moisture.

Replens is different from other lotions or lubricants because it contains a patented bio-adhesive ingredient that allows it to attach to dry, compacted cells and deliver continuous moisture until those cells are naturally regenerated (about every three days). Replens leaves vaginal tissues hydrated and feeling rejuvenated. You can use it with a silicone-based lube.

It pumps up severely atrophied tissues. Simply apply Replens a couple times a week to help alleviate the feminine discomfort associated with vaginal dryness. It might need to be used several times before you might feel the difference. This is recommend for women who have had breast cancer. Always talk to your doctor first.

Premarin Conjugated Estrogen by Pfizer:

Premarin is a purified orally bio-available female sex hormone isolated from pregnant mare urine or synthetically derived from plant materials and is used to treat symptoms of menopause such as hot flashes and vaginal dryness. Note that it can only be used for a short period of time.

Osphena:

Osphena works like estrogen in the lining of the uterus, but works differently in other parts of the body.

The Little Pink Pill: Addyi

Known as flibanserin or Addyi, its brand name, this drug changes the levels of three chemicals in the brain in ways that are sup-posed to enhance libido, although no one knows for sure how it works. It is to be used only to treat a specific condition in **premeno-pausal women** called hypoactive sexual desire disorder (HSDD). Women with this diagnosis have experienced a loss or decrease in sexual desire. The loss causes marked distress or interpersonal difficulty and is not due to another medical or psychiatric condition, problems within an intimate relationship, or the effects of a medication or other drug.

Hormones and Osteoporosis

Vital hormones such as estrogen and testosterone promote bone formation and regulate bone reabsorption, and when those hormone levels drop, osteoporosis can occur. At puberty, bone production increases dramatically, producing the growth spurt of the early teen years. This effect seems to be driven mostly by estrogens, the "female" hormones, in both boys and girls.

Near the end of puberty, androgens, the "male" hormones, increase in both women and men. The androgen surge fuses the bone growth plates, with the result being that the bones can no longer elongate. Young adults generally maintain a steady-state balance in which new bone formation is nearly equal to bone resorption.

Sex hormones also remain at roughly steady levels throughout young adulthood and early middle age. After about the age of 35, however, the total amount of bone in the body begins to diminish. In women, the process begins fairly sharply with the onset of menopause, when estrogen levels drop dramatically. In postmenopausal women, bone is lost both from the inner and outer surfaces of bones, as bone resorption by osteoclasts exceeds the already reduced new bone formation by osteoblasts.[7]

Risk vs. Rewards:

Be willing to try anything that will improve your sex life, if you want it improved. There are side effects no matter what we take. The choice is always ours. My decision came because I was so miserable. But I believe in the quality of my life. I found tools and created my own Toolbox. I was not going to stop enjoying and wanting sex because my body was changing, especially if I could make it better.

Chapter 8:
Sex gets better when you're older!

You're having sex? You've got to be kidding! I have great news for everyone, young and old. Everyone fears getting older. Some people quit celebrating their birthdays because they think their lives will end when they reach 40. Sex doesn't stop as we age. Well, it doesn't have to.

SEX is happening in retirement communities, assisted-living facilities, and nursing homes. You might imagine them reading quietly, doing crossword puzzles, playing bingo, maybe even playing shuffleboard. Think again. Think about sex—unsafe sex. The Department of Health and Human Services released a little-noticed report on Medicare a few months ago that had this startling statistic: In 2011 and 2012, 2.2 million beneficiaries received free sexually transmitted disease screenings and counseling sessions. And more than 66,000 received free H.I.V. tests.[8]

The number of Medicare enrollees who took advantage of free S.T.D. tests is about the same as the number who received free colonoscopies to screen for colon cancer, amounting to only about 5 percent of all those on Medicare. Numbers from the Centers for Disease Control and Prevention show rapid increases in S.T.D.s among older people. Between 2007 and 2011, chlamydia infections among Americans 65 and over increased by 31 percent, and syphilis by 52 percent. Those numbers are similar to S.T.D. trends in the 20 to 24 year old age group, where chlamydia increased by 35 percent and syphilis by 64 percent.[9] It is concerning, indeed, because apparently we think old people are dead inside well before they are—you know—actually dead.

One reason for this is that older people are living longer and are in better health. As a result, they are remaining sexually active much later in life. Several major surveys, including the National Social Life, Health and Aging Project and the National Survey of Sexual Health and Behavior, report that among people aged 60 and older, more than half of men and 40 percent of women are sexually active.

Also, retirement communities and assisted-living facilities are becoming like college campuses. Cram a lot of similarly aged people together and things naturally happen. I mentioned these numbers to a friend, and she was not surprised. She told me that when her father moved into an assisted-living facility, within 30 minutes three women came by to introduce themselves—and it wasn't to compare Medicare pharmacy plans and premiums. They were checking out the goods. I love it!

Researchers found that the residents of these facilities do want it acknowledged that they have needs, and they also think their doctors should be more proactive about tending to that part of their lives. Often there are no real, formal policies or guidelines in place to address issues of sexual relationships among the elderly. And there are legal complications in some cases, like needing to establish that someone is mentally competent enough to give consent.[10] This is my opinion. Their children are disgusted that their parents are "doing it." And if these parents should decide to marry in the nursing home, their children's inheritance may become an issue. I bet these kids don't have a good sex life themselves. That's just my opinion. Let's stick to the facts.

Surely it is hard to balance the needs of the patient with the responsibility to make sure they're taken care of, but it cannot be a question that is dodged altogether or else, the researchers argue, residential facilities will be guilty of "stifling their autonomy and personhood."[11] There's going to need to be more action taken on this—particularly as the Baby Boomers get older and start piling their lusty bodies into nursing homes in record numbers.

As much as some of us may prefer not to think about people older than us having sex, that doesn't mean they shouldn't be allowed to get down with whomever they damn well please—between their checkers games and knitting circles.

I'm glad they are having sex—oops, I mean we! Women get up in the morning and, rather than just hang around in their jammies, get themselves all prettied up. They put on their little pearls, comb their hair, put on a nice frock, and off they go down the hall—walker and cane will travel. I think their number one concern is intimacy, feeling close to another person, and let's not forget skin hunger (please see chapter 17).

It's never been easier for older seniors to hook up and enjoy good sex. Now they have dating sites for seniors, and besides that AARP now sells sex videos and sex toys. In their last booklet they had three different types of vibrators for sale! There's a lot of sex going on in retirement homes. More and more assisted-living facilities are selling condoms in their gift shops.

Sex gets better when you're older. No, I'm not asking you to wait till you're in your 70s to have better sex. That's not what this is about. What I'm saying is the reason it gets better is because we don't have to worry about the kids, and we have much more privacy—that is, unless the kids move back in with us. Personally, I moved without telling them just so they couldn't come back home. I know, I'm a terrible person.

Things just change when you get older and I would definitely say especially over 45 or 50. There comes a time in your life when you're more at ease with yourself and the world around you. Worries that you're not a size two are not so important. It's no big deal if you have wrinkles on your face or your belly isn't flat. We become much more relaxed in just about everything. The tensions and performance anxieties and expectations that permeated our minds when we were 30, 35, and maybe even 40 seem to all but disappear for both men and women. Making love, just having fun, and enjoying each other is much more essential. We can laugh at the silly kids today with their tattoos and piercings all over their bodies, their obsession with washboard abs and one percent body fat. I'm thrilled not to be a part of that generation.

Why do we think that sex is just for young people? I'll tell you. Advertising. When you think of older couples having sex, bumping and grinding and hugging and kissing, what comes to mind is disgust. Could it be because people having sex on TV and in the movies always have those supple, smooth, tight bodies, and are perfectly tanned, with six pack abs and no cellulite, wearing those pretty little white lacy panties? Do you ever think those same actors had body doubles do their nude scenes, or were Photoshopped to look perfect? I do not know about all of you but I have judged myself harshly because I didn't look like HER. I believe it's called brainwashing.

Let's look at television and books. When you see older couples, you see them walking hand-in-hand, gazing into the sunset. What you never see portrayed is them sharing a passionate embrace—an older man's hand sliding down the woman's back to caress her ass. Ah, but they do. Trust me! And I must tell you that older people do all of those things and more. They just don't find a need to brag about it or post it on Facebook. (Only in our country's most recent history have we seen anything skewed toward "older" couples— Viagra, Cialis, Levitra. Do you wonder like I do why the couples are sitting in bathtubs?)

Let's assume you're 65 or older. We have passion and sex drives. Having sex may be somewhat slower and not quite as often but, I can guarantee you, it gets better and better as you age. Especially if you have been with your partner for a long time, and a little added toy can't hurt (see chapter 12).

If you want to spice it up a bit, there are instructional videos recommend by AARP Sinclair-institute.com. There is also www.evesgarden.com.

This web site is designed by women for women. Just something to think about. One more thing: If your man is slowing down there are a few things that you can try. For example, AndroGel for low testosterone helps with low energy and libido.

Here's some more information for you to ponder. Is your wine glass still half full?

There is more money being spent on breast implants and Viagra today than on Alzheimer's research.

Lifestyle drugs—chiefly Viagra—are costing General Motors $17 million a year, and the cost is passed along to car, truck, and SUV consumers. The blue pill is covered under GM's labor agreement with the United Auto Workers, as well as by benefit plans for salaried employees.

GM executives estimate health care adds $1,500 to the price of each vehicle but they do not break out how much of the premium is caused by erectile dysfunction expenses. GM provides health care for 1.1 million employees, retirees, and dependents, and is the world's largest private purchaser of Viagra. GM recently raised the co-pay for erectile dysfunction drugs to $18 under a new agreement with the UAW. The company has also paired benefits for salaried workers.[12] Neither Ford nor Chrysler will disclose the amount spent on erectile dysfunction drugs.

Does this mean that by 2040 there will be a large population with perky boobs and huge erections and absolutely no recollection of what to do with them? Knowing women as I do, we will not let something go to waste. At least we will be able to use our boobs as floaters in the pool.

Women have shared the following stories:

Luisa: "Men over the age of 65 who have not had a consistent sex life, either because they are alone or with a partner that no longer wants sex, lose the connection with their lower body part. When they have an erection, they know it. But when they stop having erections they seem to disassociate themselves from their penis. They kind of like the feeling of being touched, but they do not seem to know if they are ejaculating. You almost have to tell them what is happening and get them to focus on that area and letting the sensations in. I have done this with my man and it seems to work. I just do stuff to him and he becomes more aware of the feeling. It also helps to talk sexy: You're coming now; oh that feels great—stuff that helps to get them connected and helps the brain engage. Oral sex also plays a huge part in our lovemaking."

Martha 79, Ralph 83: When they were younger they had sex three to four times a week. She was a novice about sex; he taught her everything. But things changed as they started to age. At around age 68, Ralph said things didn't work so well. He was unable to maintain an erection, but this did not stop them. They worked out a way to enjoy themselves without intercourse. It includes a lot of foreplay, but then he is able to somewhat ejaculate. She will get really aroused and then will use a vibrator. They are both good with this arrangement.

Jennifer 74, Jeremy 88: Jeremy is unable to have an erection. They also found a way that works for them. Hugging, kissing, and oral copulation. And toys.

Irene 81, Bill 82: Bill died last year; however, up until a week before he passed, they were having sex once a week.

The famous physicist Stephen Hawking was asked how he could have fathered three children while suffering from debilitating Lou Gehrig's Disease (ALS). It's reported he said that the sexual part of the brain was not affected in the same way that all the other motor skills were when he got ALS. Aha! The brain, after all, is the biggest sexual organ in the body (see chapter 14).

I really do see from my own experience that, as I get older, sex is more connected to how I am feeling emotionally. When I was younger I could be horny and go for it, no matter what, but now, more than ever, it depends on how the day has treated me, as well as the attitude my partner and I have towards each other at any given moment. It also has to do with trusting and feeling safe with my partner.

Chapter 9:
"Slip and Slide" Lubrication

Pain and discomfort during vaginal intercourse becomes a big problem for women after age 40 and during menopause, especially if you have had children and/or any bowel problems.

As a woman's estrogen level gradually decreases after her prime childbearing years, the vaginal cavity becomes drier (even when the woman is sexually aroused) and the vaginal

walls become paper thin. Our bodies gradually decrease the amount of natural lubricant,
making penetration and the motion of the sex
act painful. In addition, the walls of the vagina
and labia minora become sensitive to sperm.
Because of this one-two physiological punch,
many women over age 40 don't want to have
intercourse, mainly because it stings and hurts.
Some women put up with the pain silently
while others withdraw physically from their
unsuspecting partner. Then come the excuses.
The problem is no one wins in this situation.
This common physical change in women can
threaten the very existence of a relationship. It
takes a toll on them and us.

Bestselling author on relationships, Dr.
John Gray Ph.D., who wrote *Men are from
Mars, Women are from Venus*, observed that
"resentment in men in a marriage or cohabitation is temporarily washed away for men
when they enjoy regular sexual relations in a
committed relationship."[13] If the woman can't
physically have sex due to the side effects of

natural aging, the well of anger in her male partner will build up as the sexual contact declines. The relationship will shift from one of romance to one of conflict. The marriage or cohabitation can come to an abrupt end over this physical issue.

Everything takes a little bit longer once we're 40 and up. It's not our fault, it's Father Time. (Ever notice Father Time is a guy? Figures!) Our body changes so much once we start menopause, and our sex lives really can take a hit. Taking 20 minutes to reach an orgasm is not uncommon, and then that's only if the sun is aligned with the moon and stars, and he took out the trash.

After menopause, our drive really slows down because of the lack of hormones. Having sex becomes just too much damn work so why bother? Off to sleep we go, and I might add, unfilled. We just file it away. But there is good news. One of the greatest tools we have to combat Father Time is artificial lubrication. We are born with natural lubricant but as we age the body produces less and less. Simply put, if we're over 40 most of us aren't well oiled, and sex can be painful. We might want to consider going to bottled lubrication once we see we have a problem. I have read quite a few books written by doctors on "my" sex life. One chapter in a doctor's book was on painful sex. Five whole pages told me about the pain but not once did he suggest using lubrication.

When well lubricated, the clitoris is our hot button and penetration usually feels really good. The only function and purpose for the clitoris is to bring joy and pleasure to women. There are 8000 nerve endings in the clitoris. That is more than any other organ in our body. Guess why? To play and enjoy! We need to get wet and wild with lubricants.

True Story: Sue is 63 and had a hysterectomy three years ago. She complained to her doctor about painful sex and that she and her husband had not had intercourse in years. He told her to use olive oil. End of discussion. This is not the first time I have heard similar stories.

I gave her some silicone lube. I can say they are both smiling now and next they want to try a toy. YAY!!! The end of a dry spell. There a 100 kinds of lubes on the market for us to try and see what's best for each of us. Most good lubes run about $15 To $25 for 4 ounces. But a little dab will do ya!

Lubes are a personal preference. There's water vs. silicone, warming vs. cooling, flavored. Today manufacturers are listening to the wants of their end users and improving the ingredients. The number one lubes at the time of this writing are System JO, Ride, Sliquid, Waterslide (Earthly Body), and PINK. Let's take a look:

JO Silicone. I have tried a lot of lubes, and my favorite is System JO. It's a pure medical grade silicone. The best things about silicone is that it doesn't grow or hold bacteria, it doesn't stain the sheets, and it cannot be absorbed into the body. This means that while you're having intercourse you stay slippery longer. If you have not used a lube before, a little bit can go a long way, JO has no taste and is not sticky. Also, they have special lubes for anal sex, so there is something for everybody.

Sliquid: Sliquid Naturals. There are 13 different personal lubricant products in the Sliquid Naturals line, which means there is (at least) one for everyone! Sliquid Organics takes the most popular items from the Naturals line of personal lubricants and infuses them with Certified Organic Botanicals. Each hand-selected botanical, like hibiscus, green tea, flax, and aloe vera, is chosen for its skin conditioning properties. Sliquid H2O is their simplest, purest water-based personal lubricant in the line, and is the core formulation for all of their other water-based lubricants, with only 5 simple ingredients! Each product also uses the highest amount of post-consumer recycled materials possible in the packaging.

Ride Silicone. Ride Silicone is the flagship product for Ride Body Worx, and is a highly concentrated premium blend of medical grade silicone. This personal lubricant is ideal for all erotic sexual encounters, from sensual massage to safe and comfortable anal sex. Ride Silicone is 100% waterproof. I always recommend silicone because of its safe properties. I have never had it stain the sheets or burn. Most importantly you do not have to stop having fun and reapply lube.

Water Slide. This features natural carrageenan extract (from red algae seaweed). It is a safe and gentle lubrication with pure and simple ingredients. They stress natural ingredients. It contains no silicones, petroleum, parabens, sticky glycerin, or preservatives.

PINK. Designed specifically for women and their intimate needs, Pink® Silicone Lubricant is fortified with aloe vera and Vitamin E, providing restorative and healing properties. This light, unscented, and flavor-free formula is also hypoallergenic.

H$_2$O-based lubes. These do not last as long but some women prefer them to anything else. They are less expensive. But then you have to use more and apply it more often.

Jafra Almond Oil. Even though it is colored and oil based, I find it's a very nice massage oil even on the clitoris.

Back in the Psychedelic Sixties the late Hollywood star Natalie Wood was said to have received the surprise of her life when she jumped into a hot tub filled with champagne. It sounded sexy but the alcohol in the champagne actually burned her genitalia! My rule of thumb is the more bland the lube, the better.

One thing I found out from my friends and from my own personal experience is that KY Jelly lubes can be expensive. They are very sticky and you have to use them over and over again. Good for KY but not for sex.

The problem with petroleum-based lubes is the mess and the staining. Flavored lubes, like strawberry, lemon kisses, chocolate etc., are mostly made with a sugary substances (watch out for yeast infections) and colored dyes. If you're sensitive, it's going to burn. That's a big turn off. But try them and find the one you like and that works best for you.

Also, never buy a lube or a condom that contains nonoxynol-9. The properties in this solution are a cleaning agent and can really irritate and burn the thin walls of the vagina. Also lubes that burn can increase your chances of infection.

You can buy some of these from your local drug store, but you have to go online for the really good ones. You will find a link to my favorites on my website. Always read the ingredients.

One more thing about lubes: They are fun to put on each other. They're also a great way to touch yourself and to start to learn to get yourself ready for a toy or a boy—you pick!

Put a small amount on your fingers and rub it gently around your clitoris. You will feel yourself get hard; yes, the clitoris gets hard just like a penis. Speaking of penises, do the same for him. Put a small amount around the head of the penis and slide your hand up and down his shaft.

Lubricants are smooth and silky and a great tool to start playing and touching. They make for great and easy foreplay. The prices range from $15 to $25, but they last a long time.

Chapter 10:
The dirty word:
MASTURBATION

Say it out loud: *masturbation*. A lot of us do it, but many won't talk about it. I'm asking you, Why? By now you should know I will talk about anything. You are probably thinking, "but why this?" Because it's all about being ashamed that we do masturbate. Or that we want to.

I almost peed my pants laughing when I read over this chapter after I wrote it. It's a good thing I didn't have a glass of wine in my hand because I probably would've spilled it all over myself.

In the years that I have advised women, hang ups about female masturbation seem to be another taboo we have to overcome. So many of us have been taught by our parents, the culture, and our religious backgrounds that it is wrong to masturbate. To many it feels dirty. Good girls don't do such things… do they? Here's a newsflash: it isn't dirty, all kinds of girls do it and it's nothing new. Your great grandmother was doing it! Using some sort of device, whether a finger or an outside device, to bring about a climax in a woman has been going on since the late 1600s. Well, recorded and written down, anyway. Actually, in Egyptian time, they used smooth stones that were a phallic symbol. They also used sea sponges up in their vaginal track to keep from getting pregnant. And they had wine, too. Women are very resourceful.

The book, *The Technology of Orgasm,* reveals what doctors believed in the late 1600s.

Doctors were manipulating a woman's clitoris to reach an orgasm to stave off hysteria (which was merely a really bad day). No, I'm not kidding! In the late 19th century, it was physicians who, suspicious of the pleasure women had in masturbation, condemned it or questioned it. When Havelock Ellis wrote the synopsis of what most of his illustrious predecessors had to say about female sexuality, he stated he thought it likely that masturbation was more common in women than in men. He thought that all single women, including the divorced and widowed, masturbated. This concerned him and his colleague, Smith Baker. Baker believed that women who masturbated caused marital diversion. They were very concerned about females who were married and masturbated because that brought into question whether there was marital bliss in coitus.

The sewing machine, particularly the kind with two foot treadles operated alternately, was thought by many 19th century physicians to be either the cause or the means of masturbation in women, a concern also expressed about the bicycle. According to Kraff-Ebing, the French writer A. Coffignon thought that the power of the sewing machine was such that heterosexual women could be turned into lesbians by "excessive work" on them. Also in this same book they said nearly all female disorders or related symptoms, such as adding alcohol to your coffee and wearing a tight corset, could be attributed to masturbation. Similarly, Thomas Low Nichols considered masturbation a major source of pregnancy complications.

No wonder we all have some skewed thoughts and feelings about sex!

The sad thing that I have found in all of my research in the last 10 years is that a lot of these attitudes about women's masturbating and/or climaxing have not changed much. What in the world are they afraid of? I just don't get it. But I can tell you one thing. It's not going to stop me. That's for damn sure. And I sure hope it doesn't stop you from exploring your sexuality and having a good sex life, with or without a partner.

Guilt & Pleasure

Guilt and pleasure are competing values. We can't win.

It's my experience with women over 40 that guilt and pleasure rule us with a heavy hand. Back in the day, if a woman expressed an interest in sex or enjoyed it or wanted to try something different (because girls talk), there was an undercurrent she was naughty or doing something wrong or she would be asked (in a loud voice), "How did you know about THAT?" We kept our mouths tightly closed because otherwise we would be considered whores. We all believed that sex was a man's need, it was for their enjoyment, and we were to be available for them. Above all, if some of our women friends bad-mouthed sex and we popped up and said we might like it, whoa! The scorn of the devil in their eyes!

Once upon a time, long long ago, there was Dick and Jane. Dick wanted to see if Jane had what he had. He said, "I'll show you mine if… " you know the rest of the story. Then he wanted to touch it. Standard curiosity for children.

The kids are about to touch and feel and mother walks in and yells, "What are you two doing? Dick, get out of here!" Jane gets a spanking and is sent to bed and told she is a bad, bad girl. Meanwhile, Dick didn't get in trouble because Jane's Mother would die of shame if she told Dick's mother what he was caught doing. (Please also see chapter 18.)

More True Stories:

Robin Lynn, a 68-year-old woman, said she had never masturbated. Then she recanted, and said she tried it once when she was a teen. She sheepishly admitted she didn't know how and felt guilty about it. Why guilt? She didn't know but she knew it wasn't right.

Jane, a 50-year-old married woman, revealed she didn't know how her body worked, had never even looked at her vagina, and had never ever had a climax. She said she tried to masturbate but didn't think she was doing it right because it was a strange sensation, so she stopped.

I have hundreds of stories like these and they are all akin to each other: guilt, shame, and pleasure.

My personal opinion is that many men and many religions do not want women to have JOY. I believe many in the Catholic and Protestant churches use Bible verses to control the expression of our sexuality. And just look at how some religions enslave our sisters to the point of being stoned to death if they look a man in the eyes who is not a member of their immediate family. Foot binding was outlawed in 1997, but in the outer regions of China it is still going on. There is still female genitalia removal in some African tribes to keep women from having pleasure, and to keep all the pleasure for men. I beg your forgiveness. This is a hard read, but it is a true fact for women in Africa and other regions.

The real story is women and young girls hear this kind of stuff and it seeps into our minds. We are affected by these types of stories by osmosis. It is 2015 and this is still going on in other countries.

I feel that most men do not feel shame or guilt about masturbation like women do. To them it's a natural part of being a guy. Many men talk about it all the time. They touch themselves openly any time they want; in sports, on television, and at work, with no thought whatsoever as to where they are. Also, have you noticed that men can talk about masturbation and how often they do it and when they started? Remember the Seinfeld episode "The Contest"? Guys have a host of public names for their penis: cock, Johnson, Big Wally, the boys, my junk, junk in the trunk, the Man, the pounder, my sausage, the hammer, daddy's here, and the firehose are just some examples. It's like their penis is another person, a complete entity.

I'll stop here. If you want more names for men's private parts, or women's, you can go to the Urban Dictionary (http://www.urbandictionary.com/) and see many more. The point is that men are proud of their genitalia and of masturbating, while women are told to cover up the fact that we are just as sexual as they are. The play "The Vagina Monologues" was a sensation because it violated our society's taboo against talking about female genitalia and masturbation. But the taboo still remains.

With this smothering mindset of religion and men it is hard for women to overcome the irreconcilable difference between guilt and pleasure. The good news is it can be conquered. I think—and hope—the younger generation will not have as hard a time as we did. Remember, the clitoris's only purpose is to bring pleasure to women. For the religious set, you can't deny that God designed it for pleasure. And pleasure isn't just for men. No I'm not man bashing. These are the facts in our world today. But it does affect our thinking at a subconscious level.

Chapter 11:
How to Masturbate

Kevin Plank is the CEO and founder of a leading manufacturer of sports performance apparel, footwear, and accessories. He argued that we know more about the cars we drive than our own bodies.[14] You can turn your car on and it tells you immediately how much gas you have, what your tire pressure is, how many miles you've traveled, and what radio station you're listening to and who is singing. A lot of the time the majority of us do not know how our bodies work, what makes them work, and we don't know how we feel. I completely agree with him. I lived in the dark about my body for a long time, and I know I'm not the only one.

Let me tell you about Raylene. She is a 40-year-old woman. She did not have a good childhood; however, that did not stop her from being married and having a good life and lovely family.

She confided to me that she had never had a climax and didn't know what to expect but felt there had to be more. Raylene's husband would ask her how it felt and she would say fine, good. And it would be fine. She enjoyed the closeness of the hugging and kissing, but she had no feelings beyond that. I told her pretty much what I wrote here about how to masturbate. She tried it several times until she reached the climax she was seeking. Then she said, "Holy moly, this is great." She was able to share this with her husband and he understood. I can report that for the last 15 years they've had a very different sex life and are both extremely happy. It added a new dimension to their relationship. It took a lot of courage on Raylene's part. It's hard to change. But she wanted more and thought there should be more—and she got more! It doesn't mean there weren't some obstacles to overcome, but it worked out just fine because she followed directions and her body performed well.

Inquiring minds want to know… how do you masturbate?

Let's pretend. When you bake a cake, even if it's a box mix, you have to follow the instructions, right? Correct!

Let's leave all the shoulds and shouldn't's, the do's and don't's, the what if's and the "Oh my god, I'm so guilty" feelings aside. Leave them in the kitchen sink and walk into the bedroom. We need to practice letting go of the daily worries about husbands, boyfriends, kids, our job, the laundry that needs doing, and so on.

It is very difficult but not impossible to let them go and to be open to our sexuality. In our fast-paced world where we get pissed off that it takes a whole minute to heat coffee in the microwave, it will be hard to let go, but you can learn to do so over time. Be patient with yourself. And yes, you do have the time.

Of course I'm assuming this is something you want to learn how to do because it really is something we can learn. There are several ways to begin. Let's turn down the lights and close the curtains so you feel a sense of privacy.

The first thing I recommend is to put a mirror on the floor (a fairly good-sized, hand-held mirror), stand over it, and take a look at your vaginal area. Spread your lips and take a look. Squat down for a different look. Touch her and say hello to your pleasure center. (Remember, you're checking out your engine!)

I would suggest putting on some soft or seductive music, lighting a candle, or doing something to help you to relax. I would also have some nice soothing lubricant on hand.

This might be better with wine, too. Let's begin your romance novel, let your mind wander. *Fifty Shades of Gray*. Anything that turns you on.

Start with putting oil or lube on your fingertips and gently touch around the outside of your labia and your lips inside and out, and see how it feels. Move to the clitoris which is the very top where the two lips come together,

then move on down to the inner part of the lips around the opening of the vagina, and just experience the feeling—get to know yourself.

If you get scared or frightened, don't give up. There's no right or wrong way, just experiment. You are going on an adventure. An amazing adventure. It's okay, stop for a minute, take a deep breath, and relax, but keep going forward. Don't be frightened if the feeling starts to intensify, especially if you're not accustomed to touching yourself. This is critical. Don't give up. There's no right or wrong way, just experiment.

Take one or two fingers and massage your clitoris—it will come out of its hiding place. Touch, squeeze, pinch, and rub her fast or slow. Feel the changes that it makes and pay attention to how all parts of your body react to this new excitement. At times you may want to stop because you're not use to this feeling. It's okay to pause, but don't give up. Try putting a couple of fingers into your vagina. This will let you know how your body is responding to the stimulation. Do not be surprised if you start getting wet—that's exactly how it is supposed to be. If you're menopausal, use some lubrication.

If you have a little toy (see next chapter) and want to try inserting it at this time you can, or you can put another finger into your vagina and continue to touch the head of your clitoris. If you've gotten this far, you might want to slow down and give yourself a break, then let it build back up again. This will intensify your climax.

You may feel the need to speed up the movement of your fingers or be a little rougher—you won't know what suits you until you experiment. You might also turn your vibrator up to a higher speed (see next chapter). When you climax, you will know. Your clitoris is the driving force to a climax.

There are also many different positions you might try. This, again, is your own personal preference based on your experiences. You might like to bend your back with your legs up in the air, or you can have your legs resting on a pillow at the back of your knees so that you can rest your legs and still part them in comfort. Or you may want to lay on your side and bunch up the pillows or blankets between your legs. You might want to be on your stomach or try sitting on a chair with your legs resting on the side of the bed. Most of all, see what feels good.

Many women with whom I have spoken said they started in the bathtub, letting the warm water fall down just above the top of the clitoris and slowly moving down, letting them experience a very warm and intense feeling. Make sure you get the water temperature right for you. For me, warm water is also very relaxing. The other popular bathtub accessory is the hand-held showerhead. It's fabulous. Trust me, I've tried it.

I believe that sex—intercourse, making love—is all about intense feelings. We can give ourselves more pleasure by using different sensory items like feathers, warming oil, a scarf. Trying having the scarf glide over and rub your bare nipples and between your legs. Then slide the scarf over your belly down to your clitoris. It's quite a feeling. Another way to intensify your feelings or those of your partner is to wear a blindfold. When you can't see, all your other senses get hyped to a new level. This goes for your partner too.

There are a lot of women out there (statistics say 65%-75%) who have never climaxed. If you're in that percentage, don't give up.

Your clitoris is your control button. It is the one that will let you know what you want, what speed to go, and how much you can take. The only rule is Do not quit! It's worth it. And, after all, that's why it's there. To bring you *A Little Bit of Pleasure*.

Mutual masturbation

If you're new at this, you might want to get a glass of wine while you're reading the next part!

It's very exciting for a partner (male or female) to watch you masturbate, and vice versa. People are somewhat visual, and men are definitely optical. It's how their brains work and it's a huge turn on. Give yourself approval for this. Remember, it starts in the brain (see also chapter 14). You might be uncomfortable with this at first, but once you lose the inhibition (it's not going to go away if we don't try) it's quite thrilling. Give yourself permission to start your brain working. For men, it can be so exciting to watch us bring ourselves to the height of excitement, and watching puts him or her in a fevered pitch of sexual arousal. We as women are often so afraid to show this part of ourselves to our partner because we worry what they are going to think of us, what questions they are going to ask. We doubt ourselves, saying, "What if they think it is silly? What if I breathe too hard or what if I make a noise?" Or we think, "He won't respect me; he'll think I'm a whore." Do any of these things sound familiar? Well, I say balderdash to all of it! That's just your head talking and it never tells the truth. NEVER. Well, maybe if you are adding 2 and 2.

I guess the thing I forgot to say in masturbating with a partner is there needs to be mutual trust. I think this outweighs everything. You can love somebody, but that doesn't necessarily mean you trust them. To me, trusting my partner means I feel safe and know he cares enough about me and our sex life. Believing that you can tell him what you like and seeing what he likes takes a while. Sometimes it's one teaspoon at a time. For me, trust is number one.

If you're a widow, divorcee, or single, your sex life is in your hands. You don't have to wait for a partner (or maybe you don't even want one) to have a good sex lifespan. Remember, anything's possible. You're on an adventure. This is YOUR voyage.

Chapter 12: Toys—Women, Start Your Engines!

Men are like gas engines: you start them up and they just go crazy. Women, on the other hand, are like a diesel engine. They take a little bit to get warmed up, but when they do, they will last forever.

Remember that everything takes a little bit longer once we get past 40. It's not our fault. It's a fact of life. Our bodies naturally change once we start menopause. One of those key changes is that it takes a lot longer to climax. And after menopause and with the stress of the day, our drive to have sex really slows down. Sometimes it's just too much work. "Why bother?" we think as we fade off to sleep, unfulfilled. We just file it away. But we are missing out on so much pleasure. Whether it is penetration with a finger, a penis, or with a dildo it all feels really good. However, just penetration is not the way for all of us. Some women take more than that to climax. For many of us, close is no cigar. As I said before, only inches away from the vagina, the clitoris is our hot button, with over 8000 nerve endings. The only function and purpose for the clitoris is to bring joy and pleasure to us *women*. Stimulation of the clitoris will bring you to orgasm. And that is the number one way the majority of women climax.

I am not saying that penetration doesn't feel really good. Some believe there is a G spot, some don't. The G spot is on the roof of your vagina. Like all things on our body, some are more sensitive than others. To help you find it, open your mouth and place your thumb on the roof of your mouth. If you go backwards from your two front teeth, you will find a dip ever so slight, and that's what it feels like for its cousin, the G spot. And when it is stimulated, either by fingers or a toy, it heightens the sexuality of playtime.

Exploring the wonderful world of toys is an *adventure!*

Sexual toys can be one of the most exhilarating, exciting, and fun apparatus in the bedroom.

Rachel Maines chronicled the history of women and toys like the vibrator in her book, *The Technology of Orgasm.* One of the first electric vibrators was patented by Hamilton Beach in 1902 and was later sold by Sears and Roebuck. It was in an ad called "Aides that Every Woman Appreciates." Talk about an understatement! It was a vibrator with attachments and went for $1.35. The motor was a Hamilton Beach mixer. The J.J. Duck Co. of Toledo Ohio offered the vibrator in their 1912 catalog, "Anything Electric." The prices mostly ranged from $4.95 to $11.95 and they had a deluxe professional model for $28.75. The deluxe model had a lot more attachments. That hand vibrator your grandmother had wasn't for sore necks! Today, Amazon is the largest purveyor of adult toys, offering about 60,000 items that can be ordered discretely.

The sexual toy industry is a $15 billion dollar industry. That's a lot of money for something that's done in private and rarely discussed, don't you think? Also, the toy industry demand goes up when the economy goes down.

What can the vibrator do for women? It can bring back her sex life, or create one if she never had one that was satisfactory to her. One of the very first sex toys I used came from my husband. It was called Big Red because it was big and it was red. My husband said, "This is for you." I was so embarrassed, but at the same time I was thrilled, because he wasn't a very good lover. To be fair, he was a selfish lover, but back then, I never asked for anything.

The bottom line is that Big Red and I had a great relationship.

My relationship with my husband did not suffer because he didn't have the same drive that I did and I really like sex. But I was conflicted once again. Part of me did feel guilty. But he had bought it for me, never asked me if I used it, never asked me if I enjoyed it, and never asked me if he could participate with me. So why should I worry about it? Now I look back and realize he sure missed out on a lot of fun for both of us. Just so you know, Big Red lasted a lot longer than the husband did!

Ladies, let's get those engines working again!

My belief is that we as women are more willing to accept a lousy sex life. It is sad but true. But we can sing another tune, a joyous tune, we just need a different instrument to accompany us.

This is where "The Toys" come into play. They can get our engines ready to go in less than five minutes! No more hour-long make out sessions and wrestling with our partner and ending up unsatisfied after he ejaculates and falls asleep. With toys we can take care of ourselves and still get a decent night's sleep. It sounds too good to be true, right? But it really does work. It will bring about a climax very quickly with or without penetration. In fact, after the first climax it's possible to have a second one with a partner and penetration. Also, we can discover what we like and what we don't like, which we can then share with our partner and enable our lovers to be better lovers to us. They don't have to guess what works and be frustrated. We don't have to fake it to protect their fragile egos. Everybody wins with toys! These toys range in price from just a few bucks to several hundred dollars. Here are a few of my favorites:

The Rabbit: Picking a vibrator is a personal choice, but let's start with the one popularized in the HBO drama "Sex and the City."

The Rabbit has several features. The shaft is filled with pearl-like beads, which rotate to stimulate the internal walls of the vagina. The shaft is hard and is for the vagina, giving that full feeling of penetration, while the two little vibrating ears are designed to massage and give all the attention to your clitoris. When it comes to clitoral orgasm, a bigger shaft is not better. It's all about stimulating those 8000 nerve endings. The Rabbit is one of my favorites.

The Butterfly Kiss: This toy is much smaller than The Rabbit, but features dual clitoral and G-Spot stimulation, resulting in complete and satisfying pleasure for women. The shaft of the Butterfly Kiss is curved to hit the G-Spot, which you may recall is located on the ventral roof of the vagina. It features an unbelievable fluttering-like butterfly for the clitoris with convenient controls which are easy to use. This is the ultimate in total feminine arousal. It is waterproof for fun in and out of the water.

Sensually designed, it comes in two types: a power packed 3-speed or a 9-speed with pulse action. It is a number one seller.

Finger Fun: I call this "My Personal Assistant" because once you use it you won't know how you got along without it. This toy features direct clitoral stimulation. You place the wide rubber like thing over your finger and the little curved fake finger touches and vibrates your clitoris. You are able to touch yourself while you are having intercourse. It can also vibrate your partner. Double the pleasure. It is battery operated so it can be used discreetly anywhere—in the car, on a camping trip, on a secluded beach, in an airplane under the blanket, wherever your imagination may lead you. It is perfect for a power blackout. Put it in your earthquake kit—okay, I'm kidding. Maybe… Not!

The We Vibe: This toy is really something interesting. One part, which is flat, is placed inside the vagina, and the penis can slip in at the same time. The smaller part lies on top of the clitoris. It's a win-win. It has nine vibration modes and automatic shut-off. It is made from 100% medical grade silicone, and is lead and phthalate free. Included is a satin travel pouch and charger. It is very nice for both parties or by yourself.

The Shaft: This vibrator commands power and pleasure with a smooth, firm shaft and emphasized ridges on an imposing head for repeated G-spot stimulation, along with a waterproof bullet vibe that gives waves of pleasure.

I mention these five favorite vibrators, but don't stop there. There is something for everyone and every taste: straight, curvy, bumpy, hard or soft, fat or skinny, stainless steel or glass, anal vibrators, beads, strap-on dildos, some that vibrate, some that rotate, some that do not. There are vibrators which operate on electricity and some that use batteries, and there are some that are waterproof to use in the shower, bath tub, or pool. And don't forget remote controlled panties. I kid you not! Again, anything you can imagine in your most sensual dream is there. Whatever you try, just remember that pleasure is the name of the game.

Other vibrators:

Charisma Bliss Pink 10 Function: This little pleaser is slightly curved for G-spot pleasure. It vibrates and pulsates, has top push control, is waterproof, and is easy to use. It comes in pink and black. It is 4 inches long. It's good for a beginner.

Pocket Rocket: This is the most popular tiny little vibrator on the market and it is great fun. It's definitely just for your clitoris and it can go anywhere—slip it in your purse, travel with it—because it is very quiet. It sometimes has attachments. Screaming O makes one. Doc Johnson makes one.

The Bullet Vibrator: You can nestle the bullet vibrator underneath your palm and enjoy sex in the missionary position while the bullet hits your clitoris. You will feel a slight and enjoyable pulsation.

A Vibrating Lipstick: This is a very discreet vibrator, perfect for us moms. It looks like a lipstick tube so husbands or children rummaging through our purse for change or gum have no clue what it really is. It's a great gift to give a girlfriend for a bachelorette party. You run it over your clitoris and it vibrates and helps to get you to climax.

More advanced vibrators and other toys:

Magic Wand: Made by Hitachi, this is one of the most popular vibrators. It is electric and has a tremendous amount of power, so my suggestion is go slowly and carefully because you don't want to pop your eyes out. All the reviews are pretty much the same: "Oh My

God I Saw the Light." The Wand is primarily a clitoris stimulator, but it also gives a great neck, back, or foot rub. It's perfect for beginners if you want to experiment. The only downfall is that it needs to be plugged in. If you're far away from an outlet you will need an extension cord, but it will be well worth it.

The Cadillac: This is a two-speed vibrator. It runs 5,000 rpm at low speed, and 6,000 rpm at high speed. I call it sheer bliss. It would give NASCAR a run for their money. I bet we can get over the finish line before they do! Wait! There's more. It can be a great lead into your partner's education to the world of toys because it does not look threatening. You can start the "massage" on his back and move around, down, between… you know what I mean. Remember it's an ADVENTURE!

Gigi 2: Need some help finding your G-spot? This little vibrator will help you out in no time. It has 8 different settings that are all nearly silent, so you can use it privately if need be. It is the ultimate G-spot vibrator, but it comes at a hefty price tag. Still, you can't put a price on a good orgasm, right?

Luna Beads: This is a toy that gets better the more you use it. When you use Luna Beads, you are actually giving your vagina a workout, which leads to more intense orgasms. Even if you are having orgasms regularly, you can be having even better ones. You work out other parts of your body, don't leave out your vagina by using Luna Beads.

A Pillow: This is one you probably just have lying around your home. To get a better orgasm, try propping a pillow underneath your butt during sex. This will give your man better access, and therefore make it more likely that you will have an orgasm. There are custom pillows that you can get out there for just this occasion, but really any pillow will do.

Restraints: You can also purchase some type of restraint. This could be handcuffs, ropes, a gag, or anything else. If you or your partner are the type that likes to be restrained, then pulling this out in the bedroom can add some extra fun. Just make sure your partner is cool with it, as you don't want to frighten them. The type of restraint you get will be up to your personal preference, but there are a lot of options out there. You should be able to find something you like. Remember, fun is the name of the game.

Basix Slim 7 Inch Dildo: I have to tell you about this one also. It's a dildo that is shaped like a life-size 7" penis—actually, it comes in many lengths. It's latex-free, phthalates-free, hypoallergenic, environmentally safe, and made from non-toxic materials using American-made silicone and has a suction cup base on it, so you can stick it on any hard surface like the kitchen floor. I was thinking it could be put in the shower and back up to it cowboy style. Since it is a porous material, it won't clean as well as some of the others. You should probably use a condom with it, especially if you intend to use it with other people.

Dildo vs. Vibrator

You may be wondering what the difference is between a dildo and a vibrator. Both dildos and vibrators are designed to penetrate the vagina or anus, but dildos do not vibrate. You have to move them yourself. Dildos can be curved, normally built, or shaped like a penis. They can be big or little. The main thing is they serve as something to penetrate us and then we use our own hands or someone else's hands to make it move. A vibrator, as the name implies, vibrates you to a climax. They come in many different sizes and shapes and are bountiful in the toy world.

There are several schools of thought on the pros and cons of using a vibrator versus a dildo. I present several of them to you:

1. Some feel that vibrators are too powerful for some women. They think the clitoris is way too sensitive to take all the power. But the solution to that fear is to buy one that is not going to blow the top of your head off… unless that's what you want. Start slowly.

2. Some doctors and professional sex therapists have said that if you use a vibrator you won't want to have sex with a man. That has not been my experience at all, with myself or the women that I have mentored. I have found that if I stop using the vibrator for a few days my sensitivity to a man will come right back to me. My desire for a real male sex organ does not die. Toys just serve the purpose of bridging the gap between being aroused in intercourse and actually climaxing. That doesn't mean you don't still want to have sex with your man. It just takes the pressure off him to get you to have an orgasm. And yes, men do worry about that.

3. Some people say that if you use a vibrator it will make your clitoris go numb. Really? That is not my experience.

4. Another fear is that if you use a vibrator regularly or more than once a week you will become addicted to it and you will have to do it all the time. It certainly is possible to get addicted to anything good like food, yoga, and sports. But that is not my experience.

Anal toys

If you have an interest in trying anal stimulation, Dr. Hilda Hutcherson, author of *Pleasure: A Woman's Guide to Getting the Sex You Want, Need, and Deserve*, has some good advice on this topic: Don't start out with the penis. Work your way up, stimulating the outside with a finger or tongue, then slowly use your finger to enter the anus. And then once you get used to that, you can go on to bigger and better things.

You've got to want it.

And you've got to take it slowly.

You will also need a LOT of lube for anal sex toys. You've got to rub it all over the toy, dildo, or actual penis. Then, using your fingers, put the lubricant around the anus. Go slow.

Glycerin-based lubes don't last long enough. If you use one of these, you have to stop, put more on, and re-enter. A silicone-based lubricant is going to be a lot better for anal sex. Also, there are lots of anal toys. There are anal beads. There are dual dildo/vibrators, where one goes in your vagina and one in your anus at the same time. It will also reach your clitoris if it's built like The Rabbit. One that could reach all three spots is called the Triple Threat. Most companies that you use will have similar anal toys.

A few years ago I went to the Adult Toy and Film show in Los Angeles, California (it's like an auto show but with more people). I was shocked but not surprised at what I saw. Can you imagine a convention floor packed corner to corner full of adult toys and videos? Men and women alike were there. And watching the people was a wondrous thing. As I stated before, this is a growing industry. Outside the entrance door were 6 ATM machines, with a line of 6 to 10 people deep at each machine to get cash. Yep, they only took cash to get in the doors, and it was $35 a head. If you can think of it, it's out there. Really it is!

Growth in the adult toy world is driven by developing cultural norms which are gradually shifting. For example, people's perception of a sexual enhancement pill for women went from taboo to more socially acceptable and is becoming much more popular. Now we have a pill, and it's reported that it will be put on the market on October 18, 2015. My understanding from the FDA and other information that I have read, is that it's only for pre-menopausal women, so I won't go into details in this book.

In addition to developments in birth-control methods which are decreasing part of the risk associated with sexual activity, mainstream culture from literature to TV often boosts the demand for adult toys. The bottom line is that growing social acceptance of sex appeal has made toys, lubes, and books about sex more acceptable. Just look at *50 Shades of Grey*.

Toys and Fear

Using toys in a sexual relationship or by yourself can really improve your enjoyment of sex. We women after the age of 40 have a harder time reaching satisfactory climax with intercourse or with traditional masturbation. The toys are an engine starter. Since the clitoris is the push button to revving up our great machine, I recommend you give it a whirl. You're only a buzz away from a great climax. It's worth a try.

If you try it and you like it, that's great. If you try it and you don't like it, then don't do it again. As I said before, I find toys supplement our sexual experience and allow us to experience climaxes on a regular basis without replacing our relationship with our partners.

Last week my friend, Betty, 72, called with a sad sound in her voice. My first thought was that a friend of ours had died. Nope. Her vibrator did. She was ever so sad. They have been a couple for 30 years. Now that's a hell of a relationship! Do not worry, she has a new, younger friend, BOB—Battery Operated Boyfriend.

Most Men Aren't Actually Threatened By Your Vibrator

A 2008 study from IBIS World shows that vibrators can improve ladies' sexual function beyond just giving them more orgasms. And contrary to the stereotype, most men are totally okay with that.[15]

LiveScience reports that researchers surveyed 2,056 women and 1,047 men about their attitudes on vibrators, asking them whether they felt vibrators were "a healthy part of many women's sex lives" or were "intimidating to women's partners." About half the subjects agreed with positive statements about sex toys, while just 10% agreed with negative statements. Women who had a positive view of vibrators and had also used one themselves in the last 30 days reported a variety of sexual benefits, including more arousal, lubrication, sexual satisfaction, orgasms, and less pain during sex. And, for the most part, dudes did not begrudge them these benefits. Thirty-seven percent of women thought men felt intimidated by women's vibrator use, but 70% of men disagreed.[16] Let me know what you think.

Of course, it's possible men say one thing on a survey and another in bed, but the fact that a majority of men say they have no problem with vibrators is a step in the right direction. It may well be that a small number of vibe-hating dudes are giving other guys a bad name—after all, many men would probably be quite happy for their partners to experience more arousal and orgasms. There's an interesting catch to those benefits for ladies, though. Only women who have positive beliefs about vibrators seem to use them. It makes sense that if you feel guilty or dirty for using a sex toy, or if you're worried your partner will be mad at you, it might not improve your sex life at all. I still hold to what I said. Try it, you'll like it. Then introduce your thoughts and toys to your partner. It's worth a try.

Enjoy life NOW. It has an Expiration date!

Chapter 13:
Lips + Kissing = Better Sex

"I have found men who didn't know how to kiss.
I've always found time to teach them."
—Mae West, 20th-century entertainer

What do lips have to do with better sex? A lot! Kissing and talking can be the whole big gumball in having better sex.

University psychologists have found that among people in exclusive relationships, the frequency of kissing was more correlated with relationships than sexual intercourse. Lead author of the study, Rafael Wlodarski, writing in the Archives of Sexual Behavior, observed, "You would think that intercourse would be even more bonding, more intimate, but that's not necessarily so. Maybe you have a happy relationship and you don't need more intercourse."[17]

Dr. Justin Garcia, an evolutionary biologist at the Kinsey Institute at Indiana University, concurs. He says, "We know that physical contact, specifically good quality touch, is really important for long-term relationships."[18] As writer Jan Hoffman noted, a lifestyle of kissing your partner consistently connotes a much more serious emotional dimension to a relationship than a sexual encounter.[19]

Kissing is very sensual. It is warm and inviting. Good kissing is learned, not inherited. Anyone can become a good kisser if they are willing to put a little time into improving their technique. Ego and not being honest can be a big block, so start slow. Be curious!

In the 1950s, necking was a national craze. Couples would spend hours sitting on the bench seat in their '55 Chevy parked at the drive-in theatre, just kissing. By 2015, men and women have been so eager to get to the main event they have forgotten how great the warm up act can be. If you want good sex, you need to get in the DeLorean and travel in time back to the era of hula hoops, poodle skirts, James Dean and Marilyn Monroe, Sputnik, and I like Ike buttons. For women, kissing is the perfect way to get the sexual motor running.

If your partner is not the best kisser, then I have the game for you!

ME's Kissing Game: Kissing is a pathway to intimacy.

1. Approach your partner when you two are alone and he seems to be frisky or at least in a good mood.
2. Sit on his lap, on a blanket on the grass in a park, looking out at the sunset, on

a couch, on the bed, in a hot tub, anywhere (just not when a sports game is on).

3. Give him a touch on the hand to get his attention and look deep into his eyes. Eye to eye contact can be hard, but do not give up. Do not be embarrassed, you'll get better at this. I promise.

4. Ask him to try "a different way" of kissing. This usually intrigues men, who always want to know the latest thing.

5. Start with the kind of kiss you would like. For instance, a nibble here and there.

6. Then stand back and tell him, "You try!" If he balks, tell him you read about this and you thought of him and wanted to try it. At that point, male pride will usually kick in.

7. A 20-second kiss is just warming up. Start slow!

8. Please don't rule out books on kissing. Check this book out: *Kissing School* by

Cherie Byrd. I just got it. It's kind of fun. And there's always Google. They've got lots on kissing.

I feel the warm-up time is best when we take about 30 minutes. Now, don't think I'm nuts. Thirty minutes of talking, kissing, touching, kissing all over, and more talking and saying what feels good. Most of all asking questions. See what you both like. (Remember, you need to know what you like too.) I know we all have seen hot sex in the movies when bang, 1-2-3 and she is ready and screams like a crazy cat. It just ain't so. The first time I had sex was so disappointing. What I expected was the rush of the waves, the birds in the background with a sweet sound, harp music playing, the sun setting and… you know the rest of the story. I still laugh at myself. I was waiting for that type of lovemaking, but before I could end my waiting, it was all over. And I thought, that's it? I'll pass.

Later I changed my mind. I'm so glad that I did.

I will tell you this. I still see some scenes in movies and on television and think the same way, but it only lasts for a second. TV has been brainwashing us for years. After all, they can get us to buy goods with the most stupid commercials. I have to put this in here. Advertising is geared to the 7th grade level of education and intelligence. It's no wonder we think the same thing about sex. Through the media they paint a picture and it looks like this, "Every woman has the same erogenous zones." They hook us in to watch and then we are disappointed because our partners are real people. That's why it's so hard to change what we think and believe sex should be, rather than thinking about what it can be.

To be better at anything takes a little time. Give both of you the time it takes.

A kiss burns 2 calories a minute. A Hershey Kiss is 22 calories. Mmmm. Put them together and see what happens. Just have fun. Need I say more?

Chapter 14:
Your Most Sexual Organ—
Your Brain

I'm sure most of you know this, but it's worth repeating. Our brain is our biggest hot spot. Sometimes we can't shut it off and we're really horny. But if we let daily worries like boyfriends, mothers, school, and jobs filter into our brain, they become the biggest road-blocks to a good time in the sack! I do not know why I think the things I think, but I do know I can change what I'm thinking. It takes practice and a little time. It's hard to separate the brain, but it can be done. It also works really well if you want to be with this person and you have an ongoing relationship.

The biggest public awakening regarding our minds in the sex arena was the book *Fifty Shades of Grey* by E. L. James. In listening to interviews with women and in conducting my own personal interviews, the number one statement from women was, "these books shut the noise in my head off." So we know it works. And that's the truth.

Let's go back to the Tool Box again. My brain is like a bank with an abundance of ideas, but I have to put stuff in my sex bank. Porn, reading sexy stories, talking dirty to my partner on the phone during the day, sex scenes on TV—anything I think is fair game. Nothing is wrong or bad or inappropriate if you agree to it. Whatever you two (or three or…) decide. If there is agreement, try wild and different. Just please don't put it on social media. Bad Idea!

Sharing fantasies can be great fun, and acting them out is even more exciting. Think of something you would like to try. If you do not have the nerve to try it (yet), don't give up. You might try reading out loud to each other. It's quite exciting to lay there, listen with your eyes closed, and picture the story in your head. It's deliciously enticing.

This is why being able to please yourself is so important. If I can conjure up a good sexual movie or a sexual (dirty) book which I have read and re-picture the lovemaking scene, it's a big turn on.

Please do not take offense with what I'm going to say, but the number one fantasy that a lot of women have is being taken by force and ravaged. Please understand it is not meant to hurt them, but that's how it is in the romance novels. Remember John Wayne and Maureen O'Hara in the Quiet Man? They got into a quarrel and he picked her up and dragged her into the bedroom? Well, the next scene is Maureen lying in this big fluffy bed with this big wide grin on her face and the bed frame is broken on the floor.

Another example is in the Godfather, when Sunny pushes a woman up against a door. I love that scene! He takes her, lifts her up onto himself, and they hoot and holler, almost knocking the door down. Well, that's a turn on even though the man would need a cock about 8 inches long, and he must be thin (with no belly) and strong, and she would have to be really petite, like 99 pounds or less. Trust me, I know. We did have a great laugh at trying it, even though we almost broke *it* off.

My understanding about thinking these things is that it shuts off the brain from anything else. It's pure sex and you have no control. There is no time for the good old mind to be the killjoy and say I'm tired; Billy's got soccer; wait, I have to iron my skirt for tomorrow; and on and on. It only thinks, Take me—he wants me so bad—he can't wait. And it's pure excitement.

Pick a story or a movie scene, anything that will help you. It really works. If this is new to you, it will take some time. Take baby steps. Allow your sexuality to become an expression of you, and eventually you will enjoy a better, more fulfilling sex life. With or without a partner...

Chapter 15:
Fantasy

"Ladies let's play dress-up. Get out those high heels."

Fantasies are lubricants for the brain. Our brain is the biggest sexual organ we have in our body. It turns us off and it turns us on. Let's make it work to turn us on.

We can take sexual fantasies and create a picture in our mind. This turns on electricity in our body. You can't legislate fantasies.

We can think whatever we want, however we want.

We can think about movie stars, the next-door neighbor, the high school boy washing the car; anything we want, legal or illegal, it doesn't matter if it gets your motor going. That's all that counts. There's no right or wrong way.

Last year $10 billion was spent on romance novels. That's just fantasies in print. The first so-called "nasty" books were written in the 1700s. Here in America the publishing companies wouldn't take any of these authors on in the beginning. The first truly American popular romance was published in 1972. The genre boomed in the 1980s, with the addition of many different categories. Today, North American romance novels are the most popular literary genre, and comprised almost 55% of all paperback books sold in 2004.[20] I guess they got the hint. Sex and fantasy is a money-maker. Who would have thought?

I recommend a book called *My Secret Garden* and *Forbidden Flowers* by Nancy Friday.

Nancy was the first woman to write about female sexuality and fantasies. Fantasies are an emotional starting point to get those engines going. There are so many different types of fantasies: group sex (I think that's called an orgy), people watching while you masturbate, lesbian encounters, having sex in a public place. The options are limitless. The point I'm trying to make is it's all up to you. Just because we fantasize about a type of sex we would like to try does not mean it's for real. That's why it's called a fantasy. Experimenting is simply going on a new adventure.

Why do we think that FUN can't be incorporated into sex? Who said sex had to be serious? Why do we think that sex is work? OMG, he wants to do it again?

Have you ever had a fantasy while making love or masturbating? I have. Has he ever wanted you to dress up and role-play? Mine has. Role-playing and dress up can be a lot of fun. Sometimes I have laughed so darn hard because it was the best comedy I've ever seen.

I recommend dressing up. No, you don't have to have one of those costumes that are cheaply made and way overpriced. You can make your own. I gotta tell ya, for the most part men are just excited to be wanted. Men are usually willing to let go and have a good time much quicker than us women.

I've had good experiences and bad with dress-up. The bad experiences were caused by men who didn't want to play or were embarrassed that I wanted to play. Dress-up can be a big risk. It was for me every time I tried to be a vamp. I tried it three times without success. The first time was with husband number one, the second time was with husband number two, and the third time was with husband number three. Don't beat me up because I've been married three times. I just had a bad picker. I married the same man three times but he had a different body. I fixed my picker; all better.

Anyway, back to successful dress up and high heels. When it was successful, I played a nurse. It was a lot of fun, a lot of laughter, and a tremendous intimate closeness that came from trust because I knew he wouldn't laugh at me. But it was still a big risk. Please try it. You've got nothing to lose. Being silly is a lot of fun. Laughter is the best.

Dress up is one kind of fantasy. Another way is to mess with your partner's head. Give him a call and tell him that you're thinking about him and you want to have some fun tonight and you'll see him later, and hang up the phone. You'll get him thinking like a crazy person. Then call him back a couple of hours later and say you are thinking about tonight and that you're getting ready and then hang up the phone. Nothing is off limits… nothing.

Have you ever made love in just a pair of high heels? Try it. It's way cool. My fellow called me from the shoe store one day and he asked me what size shoe I wore. I told him and he said thanks and hung up. He had me right there. CURIOSITY! He showed up that weekend with a pair of purple 5 1/2 inch high heels. I took them out of the box and said, "Are you kidding? Do you expect me to walk in these? I can't even walk to the front door in a pair of these." He said, "They're not designed for you to walk in. They're just intended for you to walk from the closet to the bedroom." Now I have them in red platform, ones that are black-and-white, and a pair with kisses all over. I'm not going to go into details, but you can understand what I'm talking about. Suffice to say we had fun.

Try this. Go into a bar and sit on a stool and order a drink. Have your boyfriend, husband, or partner (whatever you want to call him) meet you there and try to pick you up. You could reserve a hotel room close to the bar and just hand him the key and leave. This can be a lot of fun—and sex is meant to be fun!

Please don't get me wrong. There are serious moments and very loving and touching private times that are very deep. They're wonderful, but for the most part I think sex is fun. I know because for over 30 years it wasn't fun because I picked partners who didn't want to have fun nor would they try anything new. Old poops they were!

If you have young kids and money is tight, put the kids to bed and go out and sit in the car in the driveway. Smoke a joint, if you're so inclined. Or go sit in the garage after the kids are in bed. Trying making love however you want to do it. Put a blanket in the living room with wine, some cheese, and grapes, and just enjoy each other, kissing and holding and touching and caressing. Finger-play, mouth play—all of those things add to it, but don't give up if it doesn't work the first time. Be persistent! Remember, if you want a better sex life, you can have it. You're entitled to an un-limited sex life. And if you have a partner who doesn't want to play or cannot play, then it's up to you. Please remember they too can be scared of disappointing you, or scared of be-ing silly or just having fun. There are books to help you. There are wonderful candles, warm-ing wax—a plethora of stuff. Have I told you about whip cream in an aerosol can? Just know that I'm smiling.

I'm thinking of five women (just in my immediate circle of people with whom I've spoken to lately). Their husbands are not capable of getting an erection. It can be because of medication, a serious illness, drinking, or just age. They still play. They have found a way to enjoy each other's company. Again, it depends on the attitude of both partners. Attitude is the main ingredient. Fun is the byproduct!

Join the Mile High Club. That was great fun. If you don't know what that means, it's having sex in an airplane, in a restroom, or using your hands under a blanket. If you're even able to have penetration, that will be great guns. Airplane bathrooms today are so small (much smaller than they were in the '90s), but if you can slip in there together, just play around and have a good time. It's also fun walking out of the bathroom having everyone look at you and wondering what you did. It's so racy, I couldn't stand it. I smiled for a week at just the thought of it. It still makes me smile. The big secret is that the other passengers were smiling too. They were so jealous!

Let's say some Sunday you're in church, or at a PTA meeting with your husband/partner/ boyfriend/lover. Lean over and whisper in his ear, I'm not wearing any underwear! When he looks at you in that funny way, just smile sweetly. Don't say another word. Remember, men are visual and it doesn't take much to get them going. On a wonderful summer evening, go out in the backyard and put a blanket down and make love under the stars. Have a good time. But remember to shut off the sprinklers.

Try your own stuff. Try experimenting. If you can't think of anything, get the book *50 Shades of Grey*. It's fabulous for ideas. I didn't care for everything in the book, but I thought 95% of it was hot.

Reading a racy novel out loud when you're lying in bed with your partner is another very fun, exciting thing to do. The cost of a paperback is next to nothing and you can take turns reading, even if your partner doesn't want to experiment. Try putting a blindfold on him and lay there and read. Trust me, I guarantee a good reaction. Well, 75% of the time. There are some stubborn people out there who refuse to try anything new. They could be scared, or they are just old poops. I wish you luck. But don't forget you always have yourself.

Just one more trick. You can ask your man to dress up and play a cop. Or a handyman with just the tool belt on. How about a cowboy with chaps on but no underwear? Be still my beating heart! A uniform always turned me on. That's why I married a mailman. I should have aimed higher!

Try wearing underwear that makes YOU feel sexy. Or going pantiless under a dress. Start at home, then move out into the real world. It's a breath of fresh air for your puchy. Freedom. Freedom at last!

Look at yourself in the mirror. I don't care if you're overweight or not, or you're bone skinny or not; it's really not important. What you really look like is what you think about yourself inside, and if you don't feel good about yourself, then we can work on that too. Having fun in the sack is an adventure. Just do not quit.

I don't want to leave out the man's fantasy, so here are the most popular fantasies that have been shared with me: To watch his woman make love to another man, to watch her please herself, and to have two or three women at the same time. Now remember, that is in his mind, and does not necessarily need to really happen.

I believe sex is our adult Toy Box. It's made just for us, to have fun, to laugh and play. Why do we let things stop us from enjoying each other and ourselves? What if our bodies were playgrounds? Think about that! Have you heard of withholding our affections because we were mad at our partner? "If you don't do what I want, I won't give you any!" Sound familiar? In my opinion, that does not make for good relationships.

Ladies, I'll see you in the shoe department! Oh, one more thing. Wine goes well with high heels if you're not walking too far.

Chapter 16: What's YOUR Hot-Spot?

That's the question, what is your hot spot? Do you know? Is it kind of kinky and you're afraid to say it out loud or tell your partner? If you know, tell it. You can start with communication with yourself. Let's go to your drawing board, your body. Close your eyes and think, what are the certain things I like? How do those things feel? What happened that time your breath caught? If you have not experience that sensation, there is no time like Now! Okay, let's name some of them:

- ♥ Your skin—this is the biggest organ you have, and it covers the whole body, especially just under your arm and traveling down to your waist and the smooth skin on your inner thighs
- ♥ Your eyes—that look from across the room
- ♥ Behind your ears—nibbled, sucked
- ♥ Your hair—holding, grabbing, nuzzling, which leads to…
- ♥ Your lips—sweet, warm and inviting; kissing, nibbling, gently sucking (or maybe not so gently)
- ♥ Your neck—the smell; inside the hollow on your throat, a soft kiss at the nape
- ♥ Your shoulders—touched lightly or massaged
- ♥ Your ta ta's—licked, caressed, kissed, sucked, and/or pinched (clamps or no clamps; yes they make them)

♥ Your hips—big or small, that sweet curve

♥ Your ass—the very top of the crack; the skin is really smooth and sometimes very sensitive too.

♥ The back of your knees—yes really

♥ Your feet and toes (it's not for every-body)

♥ The voice—being read to

What do you like? You know the answer. Well, most of us do.

Different parts of our body make us feel warm and fuzzy where the action is. For others, you can fondle, suck, and touch for a week and a day and you get nothing.

Our breasts. I have known women who are so aroused by their ta ta's, it doesn't take much to make them climax. The nipple can be an express connection to the clitoris. The brown or pink area around the nipple (the areola) can swell when the breasts are fondled. You can have them licked, pinched, sucked, tickled, painted, bitten, or rubbed. Then there are women whose ta ta's being touched doesn't do a thing for them. Not all women like the same thing. Rule number one, everybody is different.

The ears, neck, feet, and shoulders rarely get the billing they deserve. Play with them; look at, stroke, and caress them. Be prepared for some surprises. Some regions will feel different and become red hot when you are aroused!

I love the neck, mine and his. The smell of my man's neck is intoxicating to me, but I didn't know that for a long time because I didn't take the time to really discover what he wanted and liked. Give the neck a little blow and it can give you shivers. The area behind the ears and shoulders is soft and sensitive to touch.

Close your eyes and explore all your hot spots inside, along your legs going up and down, but stopping short of your genitals. I didn't say this game would be easy!

If you like being waxed or shaved, it can be very exciting, it's like all of a sudden the skin is unencumbered, and the whole area is on steroids to sensitivity.

Massages for women are wonderful. I love them. When I have given them, the women have loved them. They say, "Wow, that was great," then in a whisper say, "I wish my man would do that." I have had a few women tell me they hate them, but not many. In speaking with some of these women, they have a hard time being touched or hugged. This can be overcome.

Honors Class: Once you feel confident you have mastered the basic game, lightly rub a blush brush, feather, scarf, powder, ice cube, strawberry, drip whipped cream or other delights like lukewarm chocolate all over yourself—or him. (The sky is the limit on what you may want to use as long as it doesn't burn, cut, scratch, or cause an allergic reaction.)

Before I forget—men and breasts: They are still man's number one obsession in women.

They just have to look—and to touch when they can. They do not care if they are young, old, big, small, medium, extra-large, or holy cow look at those!

Once you feel like you've mapped out your region, ask your partner to join you!

Chapter 17:
Skin Hunger

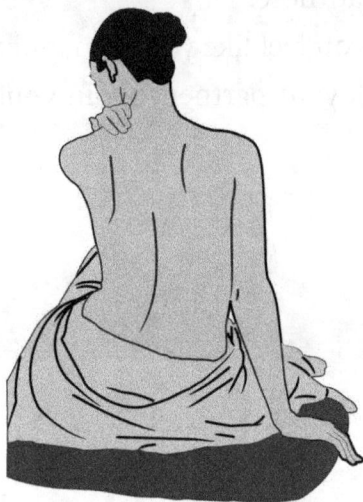

As you awaken your sensual side, you will be able to recognize the need for touch. Sometimes when that special touch happens, I feel like a puppy inside (tail wagging and all). Well, maybe not so much. You all know dogs are attention whores, how they love to be touched. They immediately roll over and beg to have their belly rubbed and their tail goes crazy. I'm a cocker spaniel. What are you?

I knew a man who went to massage parlors and prostitutes just to be touched. He told me his wife really didn't like sex and he needed human touch. He did not want an affair, he loved his wife, but not being able to feed his skin hunger was painful for him. (Also, I have been told that men will go to prostitutes just to talk. Sad but true.) The touch and warmth of the human skin is very powerful, yet we push it away because we feel something and WE decide that feeling is wrong.

I personally understand the skin hunger. I was married to a man who did not like to snuggle, and if I nuzzled into his neck or tried to spoon, it annoyed him. He said once "Are you done?" I stopped. But the hunger to be touched did not. I was pained, not only feeling unwanted, but the rejection was terribly damaging to me as a woman and sexual being. Typically we are not taught that we can touch and be touched as a neutral expression of joyful human contact.

Watch a child, they touch and hug. In my past life as a preschool teacher, my clothes were covered with their tiny handprints by the end of each day. They loved to touch me and they would hug any part they could. Kids would sit at story time and just hold hands—boys and girls—leaning up against one another. There was no one to tell them it was wrong.

When you hug someone, it's easy to tell how they feel. Some people will stiffen up; others walk into a hug, and you will feel it with your whole body. Still others hug at arm's length. How about the shoulder hug? That's where the shoulder touches but not anything below the waist. Their butts are stuck out, like heaven forbid the body parts touch. Here is an exercise: watch people at a mall or airport and see people hug. This could be your first experience of the awareness how people hug.

Please be patient with me. I will always tell you the truth. But you're going to think I just fell off the rock again. This is an actual company: *Cuddle Party*.[21] Cuddle Party is a playful social event designed for adults. They are committed to creating and maintaining safe and fun opportunities for people to learn about boundaries, communication, affection, and non-sexual touch. You can come to a Cuddle Party to meet new people, to enjoy amazing conversations, to touch, to be touched, to have fun, to practice asking for what you want, to practice saying "no" to what you don't want—all in a setting structured to be a safe place for exploration and enjoyment. You can even come to a Cuddle Party just to cuddle! Cuddle Party is a federally recognized non-profit educational organization in selected states. Its Board of Directors trains and certifies new Cuddle Party Facilitators and supports a network of Certified Cuddle Party Facilitators through its website, including ongoing training, development opportunities, and more. Before you toss your wine glass at me, I checked it out and it really is real. This is not a sex party or an orgy. They are just people who need to be touched and held.

Chapter 18:
Men are Dogs

Guys tell me that, in terms of sex, they are all sniffing around for a little action.

On the Internet, depending on which version you've encountered, the amount of time between naughty male thoughts is every three minutes, every eight seconds, every fifteen seconds, or every seven seconds. The number itself doesn't matter; it's the aura of authority, as if this were an undisputed fact backed by scientific research. I think it's spot on. I believe men are made that way. It's in their DNA. Let's not beat them up because a dog is a dog. They can't help themselves.

In contrast, sexual desire varies from woman to woman. Take your own mental temperature. How often do you think about sex?

Have you seen this? A group of women—maybe 10 or so—in a circle talking, and a man joins in the conversation. (It doesn't matter if he is good looking or not.) All of a sudden the air changes and women start primping—touching their hair, licking their lips—and a softness comes over their faces. For women, it's flirting; for men, it's sniffing. We do it too, but with a bit of class.

I always thought men knew everything. How to fix a car, defend the world, protect me, save me, make love like a movie star. (I could write a whole book on that statement alone!) I was so wrong! I had a preconceived notion about how they were supposed to be, and that idea almost killed me.

The bottom line is, I didn't stand up for what I needed or wanted, nor did I put a voice into many of the decisions of my life because I didn't think I could or I thought that what I had to say couldn't be as important as any man's. This was also true with sex. It was always about pleasing him. During the years I was married, I was never asked what he could do to please me. Nope, it didn't happen. But was it his fault? I think not. We just never addressed the subject. I tried a few times to engage us in something different but was shot down each time. That, alone, stopped me dead in my tracks from ever trying again.

Now, having an understanding of what is real, I believe these men were scared. Too scared to try something out of the ordinary. And I had no idea how to communicate with them, either. Today I offer you a way to understand and to talk about your sex life and how to make it much better. That is, if you want it! That's the key.

Okay, let's lighten up this chapter a bit. It doesn't mean anything if man is 5 or 95. I have seen them in action with my own eyes. Men are Dogs. I will give you a couple of stories. They are true… and funny.

Two coworkers, a woman in her 60s and a younger man in his 30s, were sitting at Costco having hot dogs. An older man, 90-ish, pushing his cart, using a walker, and on oxygen, approached the lunching couple. He was looking for a place to sit down. They offered the man the bench across from them. The old man smiled and with a twinkle in his eye said to the woman, "Do you know how adorable you are? Well, if I was a little younger I would be all over you like white on rice." The woman smiled and thanked him and he continued with his comments telling her that she didn't know how cute she was. The younger man had a hard time keeping from laughing himself off the bench. As the work partners left, the old man said again, "You're just adorable." She left with a huge smile on her face and thought to herself, holy cow! Wonder what he was like at 25? Probably a whole lot faster.

I think this next story is the best to make my point.

A saleslady was 42 and all the salesmen ("boys") were in their mid-20s. Five men were standing around when a long-legged blonde with a nice set of ta ta's and a perfect backside walked out of an office. She strutted past the men, without even paying notice to them. When she was out of earshot, the boys got very excited and made many verbal comments about her ta ta's and other parts, licking their lips and leering. They were in their glory; she had made their day. All five of them turned around and faced the saleslady. She said, "Hey guys, why don't you drop your pants so I can see your cocks and ass then I can judge you, just like you judged her?" One retorted with a smile, "You're gross!" I rest my case. Men are dogs. Some men can even be puppies, and puppies will lick you all over if you let them!

You must laugh. Life is too short not to!

Chapter 19:
How to Talk To A Man About Sex

Unfortunately in our busy day-to-day lives we have trouble finding the right time to talk to our men about sex, It's jobs, kids, and I'm so tired…

This can lead to frustration on the man's part, mostly because he can often sense his partner is merely obliging him and going through the motions. His friends will often make things worse by giving out bad advice such as, "she must be frigid" or "that's how all marriages end up," so he just accepts a lower level of happiness and emotionally withdraws or, worse yet, considers seeking better sex elsewhere. We feel very discouraged because our needs are not being met either. No one wins in this situation.

Men feel betrayed when the woman who seemed so sensual and sexually voracious, horny, loved to give a blow job, and just plain liked having sex with her man before marriage after marriage suddenly sets the sex timer to once every three weeks and on his birthday, with or without a bow. Men, too, want good sex but often don't know how to get around the "Women are from Venus, Men are from Mars" thinking described by Dr. John Gray, a language barrier that keeps men and women isolated and unable to please each other.

However, do we really tell them the truth? Ask yourself, do I? Are you too afraid to communicate with this man you said you wanted to spend your life with? Sometimes we are unwilling to really be truthful! Why? The main reasons are:

1. He will be mad at me
2. It will hurt his feelings
3. I'll be rejected
4. If I ask he will say no
5. My body has lumps and bumps
6. I will sound silly and he'll laugh
7. I take so long to climax, he'll get tired

Fear stops us from trying something new. Fear is a very big block for most of us, male and female. We stop ourselves from sexual pleasure all the time by listening to our fears. "Fear is a thief, it steals the joy from our lives." *Anonymous*

Our fears are often ingrained in us by our belief system, which no longer is working for us, but we still cling fiercely to them. We won't let go and are too afraid to even try. What are we afraid of? The bottom line is we think we are doing something that isn't right. According to whom? I can tell you I have been right here on this page with you so many times but I did change.

The main reason I was willing to change is that I wanted more fun and joy in my life. And I was tired of the pain of staying hurt and miserable all the time, and of settling for less. Change is hard, very hard, and the fear of changing our ways drives out any joy we could achieve. That is what we say to ourselves. Take my hand, I will help you if you want to change your sex life. (I will not sing Kumbaya, I promise.) I hear you. There are so many "what if" questions. I will try to address some next.

A few tips on talking to a man about sex:

1. Don't ever talk to a man about sex when he is distracted (i.e., his football game is coming on in 10 minutes).
2. Find a safe, private time when he is in a good mood, like when his team wins or after a good meal. Or when the house

is quiet and the kids or grand kids are asleep.

3. Say to him, "I'd like to spice up OUR sex life. Do you have any ideas?" He might ask, "What's wrong? Say, "Nothing is wrong, but wouldn't you like to try something different that would add to OUR enjoyment?"

4. Put anything he says on a written list.

5. Don't react with a frown, a smirk, or a laugh. Listen to him seriously. Everything is okay when you are brainstorming. If you try it and maybe it doesn't work out the first time, don't give up. Our partners are just as afraid as we are of change. They too feel threatened, and maybe they don't see themselves as good enough either. Laughter is a great barrier breaker. Most of all try having fun. Sex is not serious. We make it that way.

6. Don't assume stony silence means he didn't hear you. Some men need time

to process such a request. Some have their own guilt and shame issues to deal with. Don't consider a non-reaction to mean he is having an affair, and don't let it become your license to have an affair. He might be just as scared as you are of change, or fear that he might not measure up in your eyes. (It happens.) Maybe he isn't interested in these suggestions, so try another idea, such as books to read out loud in bed. You can start by reading to him from a trashy novel or Penthouse. Smile. Do not let a prudish side show. Remember, fun is the goal.

7. Rule out anything that is physically prohibited by your doctor or medication you or he are taking.

8. If the man doesn't respond, then the woman should take care of her sexual needs by herself.

Be persistent with a smile and a gentle touch. Men have feelings too. They, like us, have preconceived ideas about what a man should be, and what women think and expect of them. I believe we all fall short of what we expect of each other—and ourselves. There is a saying, expectations are planned disappointments.

Here is a true story:

I recently overheard two men talking (they did not know I heard them). One was talking about how his wife didn't want TO anymore, and he didn't know what to do. The other man said, "Well maybe she just tired of it." I butted in, "How old is your wife?" I asked. He told me she was 57. I asked if he had tried a good lube, and he told me he had tried over the counter petroleum stuff. I told him about silicone lubes and they are much happier now.

Chapter 20: Porn & Him

What to do *about porn?*

When I said men are like dogs, I really wasn't kidding. They are incredibly visual. And if you don't train them right like Cesar Millan trains his dogs, men can be easily distracted or even run away.

What I'm going to say about this subject is purely from personal experience.

I don't even think a glass of wine would help the conversation I'm about to have with you. Pornography's a big subject. And often a big secret!

As a married couple, we tried porn and it excited us. We then would put it away or we would drop it off in the video box. It was not something that was an active part of our sexual life, just something to spice up the regular sex on occasion. Unfortunately, my husband was not very adventurous.

My husband's sexual desire started to fall short after we were married. When I asked him about it he stated it was because as we got older the desire wasn't there as much (and I believed him). At the time I did not know he was into porn, nor did I have any inkling he preferred Internet porn to me.

I found out by accident. My printer was jammed and when I got it fixed, a bunch of pictures came spitting out. Pictures of women's vaginas, some shaved, some not; some were a full bush; most legs were open, but some were closed. It really was quite disgusting to me. And the biggest question I had was, "Why? Why?" He had a wife who loved and adored him. I never turned away from him.

Unless you've experienced the rage I felt towards him, you may not understand. I shook with fury. I was devastated. It made me sick to look at him and I was terribly hurt. I didn't understand. I had heard women talk about it, but I had not yet experienced it myself.

The range of emotions included betrayal and blame—something was wrong with me, again. I wasn't pretty, tall, or thin enough; I wasn't enough, period. It was always me, always my fault; if I was the right kind of woman, then maybe he wouldn't need to look at porn. I took on tremendous guilt. That's before I knew he had the problem, not me. I threw the papers in his face and stood there enraged, shaking from head to toe. He said it was an accident and that he never meant to go on that site. He always had an excuse for his behavior. He said it would never happen again. Unfortunately, I believed him and forgave him.

Our sex life began to dwindle even more and, again, I blamed myself. I would have stood on my head if he wanted to make love to me because it was all about pleasing him. I was raised to believe that the man is the head (no pun intended) of the household. He is smarter, brighter, quicker, cuter—all of those things and more. Those of you who know what it is like to walk that line understand exactly what I'm talking about.

The last straw was one morning when I was getting ready for work. I'm semi-making the bed and find a pair of women's underwear nestled in my sheets. No, they weren't mine. That's for damn sure. And again that rage boiled up in me to the point I thought I would vomit. I accused him of being with another woman. I asked, "Why didn't you just leave if I wasn't enough?" Again, all those old feelings came flooding back. Then he told me that he would masturbate with the magazine and put on the women's panties. All those years I allowed him to let me believe that I was the problem. I drove to work and made arrangements not to go home. I made sure that I took enough clothing and things I needed so I could continue to work. I was devastated and I knew that my marriage was over was almost more than I could bear. But the dance of deception continued. He begged for forgiveness, he carried on and on. He cried, "I love you more than life itself." I was desperate to hear those words even though they weren't true. He said he would never do it again. He promised, promised, promised. And I believed him. (Yes, there was a big S for Stupid on my forehead. Now, the S has since been permanently erased.)

I started therapy because I was sure that it was my fault. The marriage did end. It ended because I found out that his lack of sex drive was not because he was 60, it was because he had spent himself on magazines and ladies' panties. There was nothing left for me. He desired porn more than he desired his wife. Oh, I forgot to say his drinking had also increased and he was not going to give that up either. He was addicted and didn't want to do anything about it.

The sad part, as I look back on it, is that I ignored the warning signs and let it go on for so long. When the marriage was over I was emotionally bankrupt, withdrawn, and ashamed of my body. I felt ugly, like a piece of garbage. I went back to therapy but for a different reason. I did not want to do this anymore, put a man before me, and I kept picking the same kind of person. I was not in therapy for very long, a few months at most. I saw the light. Now I'm a damn beacon!

I have learned many painful lessons, but however hard these lessons were, they have brought me to a new, wonderful life. There's a saying by Maya Angelou, "When someone shows you who they are, believe them the first time."[22] It was a very hard message to hear, but now whether it be female or male, lover or co-worker, it doesn't matter. Once they show me who they are, I believe them. Then I get to choose if I want them in my world. Today I am much more selective with whom I share my life and friendship.

I have since cultivated great women friends. I also have a marvelous man in my life and he's never shown me anything except respect, kindness, love, affection, and complete caring. I took what I learned and applied it. It wasn't easy, but the rewards have been sensational. Don't give up on yourself. I won't. You're worth it.

The stories that you are going to read next are true. Again, the names have been changed. And these are only a few of the many I've heard. I could fill a book with just stories about men addicted to porn.

Last week I was having lunch with one of those great girlfriends, sitting in the restaurant minding my own business. There were two young waitresses. Both 19-ish, blonde, and well-scrubbed. They looked like they had just walked out of church.

I could not tell you how the conversation started with the one young woman. She said something about porn addiction and started to tell me about her brother-in-law. She said he was having a problem with watching porn on the Internet, and I added yes, that is the number one problem today in America. On the other hand, she was more upset with her sister who had kicked him out of the house. She thought her sister should be kinder and more forgiving.

What surprised me was the woman was deemed wrong for kicking out her husband who's doing something really bad.

She proceeded to tell me how upsetting this was to her and her family. I responded by telling her it is a problem and I hope that he gets some help if it's destroying his marriage. The young lady who I had never met before started to cry. I was absolutely blown away by how serious this problem was and how it was affecting her. Tears started rolling down her face as she walked away.

I have known for quite some time that we have a porn problem in America. It's the newest addiction. I believe this, and I'm sticking to it! In my opinion, watching porn is not bad. I think it can enhance a relationship or spice it up a bit. I have seen some that were so funny because they were so unreal. But when you don't have sex with your partner because they're watching so much porn, or it costs you too much money, that's a whole other ball-game. That's called addiction!

Many men won't admit there is a problem in their marriage until it reaches a crisis point or the various addictive coping behaviors that spring up become so blatant they can no longer be ignored. This is the time for women to demand not just an end to the pornography but a renewing of the entire relationship. There is hope in 12 step style recovery groups where you can talk with others who have gone through what you are experiencing. That can mean a lot. If your man isn't willing to look at his life and change, there isn't really much else you can do. Ultimately each wife or girl-friend of a pornography addict needs to evaluate her situation for herself. Life's too short to be wasting it on someone like that. In my case, I ended my marriage.

Here is a true story how porn affected one woman's life.

My first experience with pornography was when I was 11 years old. I found a magazine that showed various sexual positions between men and women. I had a very simple understanding about sex, but when I looked at the pictures I became aroused. I was not sure how I was feeling, but I liked it immediately.

I was in my 20s before I saw porn again. I was married and my husband came home with a magazine. We looked at it together and got all hot and bothered and had very satisfying sex. I really didn't care if I looked at it again but he was hooked. My husband began to get more magazines and then videos. Each time he got a new video or magazine we had to try each position or die trying.

At first it was okay. I got turned on by two women together or a scene with a man and woman. Because I got turned on he thought it was okay with me. It wasn't long before he was in a Porn Video Club receiving videos weekly, and each one was more graphic and violent. I felt much of what he watched and the fact that he wanted me to watch was degrading. I no longer wanted to participate in his new fetish.

He became consumed with the videos and sexual toys. Increasingly, disturbing movies would arrive in the mail (bestiality, fisting, golden showers, sex with lactating women, even bondage and rape scenes as well as incest). Watching this sexually deviant behavior did not turn me on, and I certainly did not enjoy engaging in it. It made me feel sick. I wanted to have sex with my husband, not a three-ring sexual fantasy designed to only satisfy him. He didn't care how I felt or what I thought, but I was too afraid to stop it.

My needs became of no concern to him and he resorted to violence to get his way. He did not believe a man could rape his wife, so he would force himself on me with these new, supposedly exciting sexual perversions. Soon he got tired of the fighting and would masturbate instead, usually on me while I slept.

He became so addicted to porn he stopped living, stopped thinking clearly, and stopped loving his family. Also, he became jealous and mistrustful. He had convinced himself that if I didn't want sex with him then I must be having sex somewhere else. This fight became a daily ritual. He would scream, "Where have you been? Who have you been with? You're fucking someone, I know it."

The last straw came after a visit from my brother. My husband convinced himself that my brother had fathered our son. He was enraged, but nothing I could say would stop his rampage. At that point the marriage was over. Sex stopped being the thing people in love do and became a selfish, addictive, twisted way to live. It destroyed his life and mine.

I was single for five years. It took a long time for me to trust another man, but with the help of therapy and good friends, I healed.

When I met my present-day husband, we abstained from any physical contact for nine months. That gave me the ability to really know the person who I was going to share my body with. I learned to talk and listen to a man.

Today there is nothing we cannot talk about—whether we agree or not. Our discussions are not a life-threatening issue. We have been happily married for 16 years.

I want to tell you a story about Steve

In my friend Steve's case, he stopped the pornography and returned to the land of the living. Everyone who faces this horrible addiction must make their own decision based on what is healthy for them. Here's his story:

Steve is a sex addict. It started at a very early age. It started very gradually and escalated to child porn, bestiality, and violent sex with all its ramifications. He stated "every line that could be pushed I pushed." He got a rush from it, and it was a big escape from boredom. But not just boredom; anxiety, worry, work, and failed dreams. Booze and food and drugs all do the same. It's just another substance. Because of the porn addiction it made him less present with his wife, his job, his family and friends. It affected his whole life. The more he watched the worse he felt about himself, which is pretty typical when this becomes your normal behavior. This could have destroyed his marriage, but it didn't.

Steve knew he personally wanted to change what he was doing and preserve his marriage, and he did get help. It saved his marriage and his life. It doesn't mean his marriage is perfect, because there is no such thing, but his marriage is healthy and whole today.

I asked him why he thought he got started on porn, and his answer shocked me because I hadn't heard it before. He said he was bored and the excitement of this new sexual desire overrode everything else in his life. The thing I respect the most about meeting this gentleman and hearing his story is that he did not blame anybody else for his behavior, especially his wife. With that, Steve was able to leave the pornography and resume a healthier life.

Porn has become commonplace in 2015 America. Once the domain of sleazy adult theatres and adult bookstores located in the bad part of town, porn has infiltrated almost every home across the nation, where it is only a TV click or a keyboard touch away.

Which state consumes the most porn? Utah, so says Ben Edelman, who analyzed subscription data from an unnamed "top-10 seller of online adult entertainment."[23] When comparing broadband subscribers, Utah comes in first with an average of 5.47 porn users per 1000 people. In second place is Alaska, with just over 5.03 per 1000. Coming in third place is Mississippi. Edelman says, "Even when I control for the income, age, education, and marital status, Utah residents still consume disproportionately more [porn] than people from other states." There are many sites that say the same things. If even the most upstanding and religious of men are getting hooked on porn, any man is vulnerable.

One of the worst aspects of pornography is the way it ruins relationships like it did to my marriage. Scientists like Joshua Knobe and his colleagues showed that porn use also changed the way men view women. Professor Knobe described the effect male porn use had on the way men perceived women as animalification—treating a woman as though she lacks the capacity for complex thinking and reasoning, but at the same time treating her as though she was even more capable of having strong feelings and emotional responses.[24]

As I learned the hard way, there is little that the wife of a pornography addict can do to interest her husband. Don't beat yourself up like I did. Male pornography users have taken artificial means to go beyond the outer limits of human beings. Marnia Robinson and Gary Wilson, the authors of *Cupid's Poisoned Arrow*, have written an outstanding article on the debilitating effect of frequent pornography viewing on men. They observed that "recent be-havioral addiction research suggests that the loss of libido and performance occur because heavy users are numbing their brain's normal response to pleasure. Years of overriding the natural limits of libido with intense stimula-tion desensitize the user's response to a neuro-chemical called *dopamine.*"[25]

Basically the experts are saying that men do not feel the ordinary joy they used to experi-ence when they first started using pornography and they don't even look at their female part-ners the same way. The male pornography user must hit bottom, break the cycle of addiction, and allow his natural desire and perception of the opposite sex to return before he can return to a healthy fulfilling sexual relationship.

The wife can use this terrible crisis as an opportunity to re-evaluate her whole marriage from the ground up. Many men feel uncon-nected to their unsuspecting spouse and chil-dren so they seek a temporary high, connec-tion, and escape from reality in pornography, lap dances in gentlemen's clubs, prostitutes, and serial adultery.

Originally, the porn business was directed towards the man because it was all about pleasing him. It wasn't about pleasing a woman. But that was then. Today you have female directors, female writers, and female stories. You have actresses who act for the female who is watching. There is a place for porn in your Tool Box, as long as it doesn't become an obsession for him.

"Sharing experiences widens one's horizons and opens up new and better ways to deal with difficulties. There is no need to solve them alone." *Al-anon, One day a time.*

Chapter 21:
Grading My Relationship

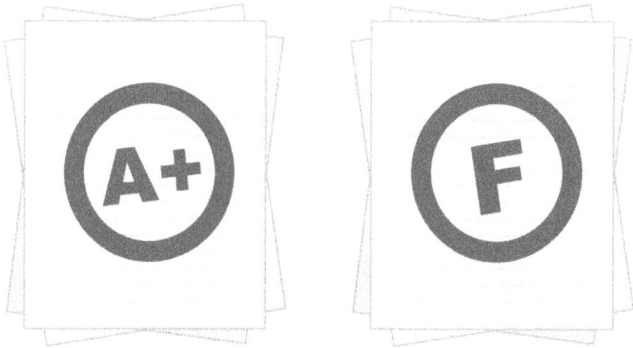

From the very start of this book, I have shared some of my most intimate thoughts, feelings, and experiences, but the one that really helped guide my life and the people who I let be included into my world now was this simple but important tool of grading my relationships. I did not receive this guide until I was in my 50s. Grading my relationships was a scary thought for me. I had to get away from all the other distractions of life and look at it in my brain. Here's a guide which helped me pick a good relationship no matter what part they played in my life or for how long.

How do you see your relationship?
1. Sexually
2. Spiritually
3. Intellectually
4. Emotionally
5. Socially
6. Economically

Grading my marriage told me there was a problem, but I did not want to do anything about the situation. I would close the door and walk away and then just bitch about my life. Sometimes I have really been blind. Even if I could have read Braille, it wouldn't have helped me. Now I realize the timing wasn't right.

And you notice what number one is: Sexually, which is the subject of this book. I always felt bad that on a scale of 1 to 10, I was a 15 sexually. I thought there was something seriously wrong with me. This just added to my pile of self-hate about who I really was. I found that changing was hard. But grading my relationships began a process that couldn't be stopped. Once I opened the book of knowledge, I read it like crazy. I knew there was hope for me and what I was feeling. I began accepting who I am and what is important in my life.

Most of the fears I faced were all in my head. (I still do not want to go there alone.) My head is the one thing that drove me, told me, yelled at me, and pointed me in a direction that was self-defeating! Today, I don't listen much to that "Darth Vader" commentator. It's been replaced with positive and healthy voices.

The question is, what level is your relationship? This is your opinion and it's the only one that counts. How do you feel about yourself when you're in the company of your partner? Do you feel pretty, smart, funny? Do you have a girlfriend or a husband who needs to put you down? A parent who always finds fault? Or do you feel stupid, inadequate, that you can't do anything right, have no knowledge of the world? Are you just plain not present? Or is he? Some women are raised with an abuser, some with a yeller, some with a person who's angry all the time. Abuse by words was the killer for me.

Being raised with indifference, it didn't matter what I did, I was just kind of nothing, transparent. Then I picked people in my life to love me with indifference. The word indifference means neutral, of no importance, little or no concern, mediocre, or average. That was me! The men I married said they loved me and they all said I was the best thing since sliced bread—but they didn't treat me that way, and that's the difference. How someone treats me is the key, not what they say.

I believed that if you just loved someone enough and you did everything to gain their love, you would get a little back. But it doesn't work that way. What I got was very little back. This is just my experience and, as hard as it is to admit, I simply wanted somebody to love me. I would beg, chase, buy gifts, and do whatever they wanted, but I got zero in return. I saw their potential and I really wanted to help them grow into the person I knew was best for them! Another sayings that changed my life is "Helping is the sunny-side of control. The other word is NAG!" Today, how somebody treats me is much more important than what they say. It's been a very, very hard lesson to learn.

I believe a father's job is to teach his little girl how to be treated by a man. I think too many men don't know this and I sure didn't. I do now. And for a little boy, the job of the father is to teach them how to be a man, how to behave towards women, and how to do the things he is supposed to do. Our children learn by watching how their parents treat each other. In my experience, the "art" of a father's and mother's job had been lost somewhere.

Here is a little fact I have found to be true in 90% of women I have worked with: How a man treats his mother is how he will be with his wife. That was 100 percent the truth for me. They all had lousy relationships with their mothers.

Let's look at each category in grading our relationship:

1. **Sexually**. How much open-mindedness is there in your relationship? Have you fallen into a rut and decided to furnish it? Or can you suggest something out of the ordinary? Are you willing to try and experiment in your relationship like trying a new recipe? If you baked a cake and it didn't taste very good, would you never bake again? No, you'd try a different way. Just don't give up. How much do you do for one another? What are you willing to do for one another? It's not always 100%. Sometimes it's 60-40 or 75-25. If I do my best that's 100% in my book.

Some marriages are bad or they are not ideal and at times there's nothing you can do to improve it. But if you stick with it, chances are you will be presented with many different choices. There's no judgment, it's just the way it is—as long as you know this is what you have chosen. Maybe it's best for all parties to stay together for now.

2. **Spiritually**. On this level I don't think it's important that you both have the same religious beliefs. If what I believe brings me peace, that's fine. If you believe differently, that's fine too, unless you're trying to push your beliefs on me. That's not okay! I don't think there's only one way to have a spiritual connection to something out there greater than myself. Everybody should have the right to believe as they choose.

3. **Intellectually**. Someone may have been to college, someone may not have, someone may be attending a trade school, some may not. I

think we have to evaluate our own personal intelligence. There are people I know who are very, very smart. They have been to college. They're great people but don't have enough sense to know when to come in out of the rain. It really has nothing to do with book learning and everything to do with your own personal skills and accepting your talents, as well as accepting our chosen partner's.

4. **Emotionally.** I was very needy. I could not make any decisions on my own. I did not trust anything I believed. It was always someone else's idea which I adopted. I was treated like a child and that was okay. That way I didn't have to make any of my own decisions. The payoff was that I remained childlike and took no responsibility for anything. My job was to cook, clean, and have babies. It definitely was not okay for me to express an opinion. A huge step in my adult married life was when I finally bought my own alarm clock and got up when I thought I should. It sounds silly but

trusting myself and becoming my own person was like labor—long and painful, but when it was done what a great baby I got—me! There is a book called *Why Do I think I am Nothing Without a Man?* by Penelope Russian, PH.D. It's a great guide into the thinking of many women like I did for so many years.

5. **Socially**. For me this is a big key. This means I can go anywhere with my partner and not be ashamed of him. I was married to a drunk. When we went anywhere where booze was served, I knew I was driving home. Once we were at a friend's house and he passed out in the soup. Wow, was that a big clue! Well I missed it, and I remained in that marriage for another five years. See how smart I was? Today I prefer someone who can engage in a dialog. They don't have to know everything. They just need to be polite, listen, and be open to hearing, learning, and allowing what someone else has to impart in the conversation. That's a good social balance for me. What is your social balance? Have you ever given thought to how you and your partner engage in private

and in public? Try it. Listening is a great tool. It's interesting.

6. **Economically.** I think we have to be pretty close in our thinking here. I did not graduate from college so I always felt insecure that I could ever make decent money, but that's not true. I earned a good salary at my job. I learned how to become financially independent which was huge for me because I was told I would never be anything or amount to anything if I didn't get married. I allowed the men in my life to manage my money (and I was always broke). Guess what? They were stealing my money. Imagine that! And I allowed it! Today, I'm responsible for my own money.

If none of this sounds familiar, that is A-okay. These categories usually cannot be filled by any one person. Make up your own grading system and see how your relationship fares. It may be just perfect for you. I'm not putting down any relationship. No matter what stage you're at, these are just ideas to get you thinking. Want to make a change? There are things you can do. See if you have the tools; if you don't, get out your Toolbox. Maybe you just need a different way of looking at the situation.

All things aside, the biggest key is communication. If you're not talking or it's really hard, start out slowly. If you're uneasy talking, mix it up a bit. Nothing is off limits, nothing.

Today, my biggest job is just to take care of myself. To pay attention to me and do whatever is necessary to make my life joyous, not in a mean or selfish way. Some days I just have to keep my mouth shut. If it doesn't affect my breathing, maybe it's none of my business. Out of that joy, I'm able to share with others. Today the ultimate reward is that I pick better people to be engaged with. Happiness is a great turn on.

The End

Paul Auster said, "Horniness is a human constant, an engine that drives the world."[26] Sex sells almost anything. If you watch some of the TV ads now with your new awareness of sex, you will see a lot of them are geared for men. They portray some pretty woman with big ta ta's who are downright gorgeous. Don't you dare compare yourself with them!

Ads for us women, regardless of our age, size, race, or religion, depict women who look like stupid housewives. Or they show her wearing a strapless top with long hair that, if you use a certain shampoo, runs back and forth and looks all sexy. Of course they don't tell you that it's not real hair. It's true. It's not real hair. It's extensions, plus five special colorings, special lights, special wax, etc. etc. etc. But wait. There is more. Your kids will love you and your mother-in law will be proud of you if your dishes are bright. And your teeth now are so sparkly, people driving by you in their car will be blinded by your brightness. Did you know that?

As I said before, the average commercial is geared for a 7th grader. They think that's our intelligence level, men and women alike. Have you watched some of the hamburger commercials? I will never forget the one where Paris Hilton was washing her car. Sex sells, but I guess that's okay as long as we don't talk about it!

Ladies, I hope my book has given you some ideas, some courage, and a new way to talk about sex. If you can talk about it, try it. If you can't, get BOB—a Battery Operated Boyfriend. I never forget my Bob. He travels well and he doesn't talk!

I've had my tragedies and so have you. Death, divorce, loss of a child. Sprinkle in heartaches and big disappointments. Today we do not have to fix our problems alone: We are sisters in this business of making a better life.

My point in sharing this with you is, don't give up. Don't ever give up! We are worth it: you are worth it and so am I. I want to see you achieve what you want in life. If it's better sex, we have the Toolbox. If you want a better education, go to school, one class at a time. I do not care if you're 30. I don't care if you're 90. The world is filled with women of all ages who keep trucking on, going forward and being happy. Just know I am your cheerleader! I have my pom-poms in my hand. You go girl!

I want to thank you for reading my book. This book was written for you. I did the hard work and I did the experimenting. I've been, I've read, I have experienced. I wish you a great sex life, if you want one.

When I wrote this book I thought of you sitting with me on the couch curled up with a blanket as we talked, our feet tucked under our butts, each with a glass of wine. I hope I came across that way to you. One of the most important things to me is that you are able to reach me to question me, challenge me, and to ask for more tools from my Toolbox. I can be reached at me@alittlebitofpleasure.com.

I want to give special thanks to Dr. Jerry, Dr. Richard, and Jim. They listened to me with the most wonderful curious minds, God bless them. Special thanks to Casey, Colleen, Barbara, and Sharon who also listened to me, edited me, helped me, and encouraged me. They are my cheerleaders. Most of all I thank the women who cried, the women who didn't understand, the women who were angry that their doctors didn't tell them the truth about what was happening to their bodies over the past 35 years, and to all of those women who are courageous enough to go forward and try something new.

I found myself in a deep, dark hole,
My preacher walked by and tossed in the bible,
My spouse strolled by and handed me divorce papers,
My parents stopped by and hurled criticism and advice.
But my friend jumped in the hole with me,
I said to her, "What are you doing here"?
She said, "You forgot. I know the way out!"

Amen, sisters

About the Author

ME Sims has had many careers over her lifetime. She was a preschool teacher, then she led sales teams and customer relations department for the world's largest automobile dealership, and has recently gone back to work in real estate. She has personal experience in unhappy marriages, raising children, and getting divorced, and quite a few years' experience being a sexual and sensual woman over 40 and despite menopause. She lives alone happily and enjoys spending time with her children, her sisters, BOB, and her real life boyfriend, Anthony.

Contact me:
Email: me@alittlebitofpleasure.com
Website: www.alittlebitofpleasure.com

Recommended Reading

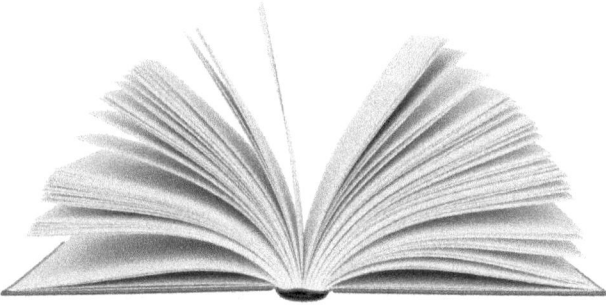

- ♥ *Men Are from Mars, Women Are from Venus,* Dr John Gray Ph.D
- ♥ *Pleasure: A Woman's Guide to getting the Sex You Want, Need, and Deserve,* Dr. Hilda Hutcherson
- ♥ *Unorthodox,* Deborah Feldman
- ♥ *The Battered Woman,* Lenore E. Walker
- ♥ *The Sexy Years,* Suzanne Somers
- ♥ *Kissing School,* Cherie Byrd

A Little Bit of Pleasure

- ♥ *Getting Off: A Woman's Guide to Masturbation*, Jamye Waxman
- ♥ *Menopause: The Silent Passage*, Gail Sheehy
- ♥ *Ride 'Em Cowgirl: Sex Position Secrets for better Better Bucking*, Dr Sadie Alison

Notes

1. http://www.brainywords.com/quotes/toler-ance-quotes.html
2. http://popcenter.uchicago.edu/data/nhsls.shtml
3. http://www.chemochicks.com
4. http://www.brainyquote.com/quotes/quotes/f/fridtjofna211342.html
5. http://www.drdaveanddee.com/headache.html

6. http://www.replens.com/FAB-Blog/Fighting-Vaginal-Dryness/34/How-Do-I-Know-if-I-Need-a-Vaginal-Moisturizer.aspx

7. http://www.lifeextension.com/protocols/metabolic-health/osteoporosis/page-02

8. http://www.sexhealthmatters.org/sex-health-blog/std-tests-for-the-elderly

9. Ibid.

10. http://www.medicalnewstoday.com/articles/247036.php

11. Ibid.

12. http://www.consumeraffairs.com/news04/2006/04/gm_viagra.html

13. https://books.google.com/ – search for "Temporarily washed away John Gray"

14. http://www.bizjournals.com/charlotte/news/2015/06/16/kevin-plank-to-stephen-curry-let-s-go-build-a.html

15. http://www.ibisworld.com/industry/adult-stores.html

16. http://www.livescience.com/16811-vibrators-sex-toys-sexual-satisfaction.html

17. http://well.blogs.nytimes.com/2013/10/28/now-a-kiss-isnt-just-a-kiss/

18. Ibid.

19. http://njbrepository.blogspot.com/2013/11/now-kiss-isnt-just-kiss-by-jan-hoffman.html

20. http://www.crystalinks.com/romance_novels.html

21. http://www.cuddleparty.com/about/

22. http://www.brainyquote.com/quotes/quotes/m/mayaangelo383371.html

23. http://people.hbs.edu/bedelman/papers/redlightstates.pdf

24. http://philosophycommons.typepad.com/xphi/2011/09/x-phi-of-consciousness-meets-pornography.html

25. http://yourbrainonporn.com/book/export/html/536

26. https://books.google.com – search for "Horniness is a human constant Paul Auster"